Activities
in the
Life Sciences

by Helen Challand, Ph.D.

illustrations by Len Meents

CHILDRENS PRESS ™

CHICAGO

Library of Congress Cataloging in Publishing Data

Challand, Helen J.
    Activities in the life sciences.

    (Science activities)
    Includes index.
    Summary: Presents a variety of experiments
involving living organisms, including growing
bacterial cultures, calculating the rate of
seed germination, regenerating animals, and
using urinalysis techniques.
    1. Biology—Experiments—Juvenile literature.
[1. Biology—Experiments. 2. Experiments]
I. Meents, Len W., ill. II. Title. III. Series.
QH316.5.C45 1982   507'.8   82-9442
ISBN 0-516-00507-3   AACR2

TABLE OF CONTENTS

CHAPTER 1
Finding Out About Simple Plants

CHAPTER 2
Discovering the World of Higher Animals

CHAPTER 3
Experimenting with Plant Processes

CHAPTER 4
Doing Things in Nature

CHAPTER 5
Working with Lower Animals—the Invertebrates

CHAPTER 6
Working with Higher Animals—the Vertebrates

CHAPTER 7
Learning About the Human Body

Chapter 1
Finding Out About Simple Plants

SEEING THE EFFECT OF YEAST ON DOUGH

Puncture an opening in a metal cover of a glass jar. Insert one end of a length of plastic tubing through the hole. Place melted wax around the hole to be sure the connection is airtight. Submerge the other end of the tube in a glass of limewater.

Combine 1 cup of flour, 1 tablespoon of sugar, 1/4 package of commercial yeast, and 1/2 cup of water. This is a crude form of bread dough. Place this mixture in the glass jar. Screw on the top immediately.

Set up another arrangement as above only leave the sugar out of this batch of dough.

Set the jars in a warm place. Soon the dough will rise in one of the jars. Remove the lids, puncture the mound of dough, and quickly close the jars again. The gas that caused the bread to rise in one of the jars escapes into the tube that leads to the limewater. Since the gas given off by the yeast is carbon dioxide the limewater will turn milky. Why didn't the dough rise in the other jar?

For additional information see page 83

DEFINITIONS

carbon dioxide — a colorless, odorless gas used by plants to make food.

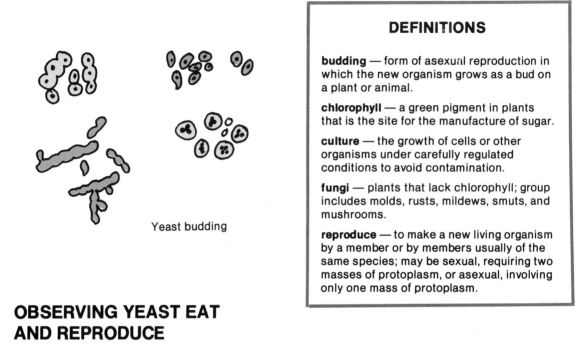

Yeast budding

OBSERVING YEAST EAT AND REPRODUCE

Yeast are tiny fungi that eat sugar and reproduce by budding. These one-celled plants without chlorophyll will break sugar apart to get energy to reproduce. The end products will be carbon dioxide and alcohol.

Mix a few grains of dry yeast in a small solution of warm molasses water. Permit the mixture to stand for a couple of hours. Place a drop on a microscopic slide. Use a cover slip, for you will need to focus with high power. Observe the buds forming. Count the approximate number of yeast in one view of the scope. Set the slide and scope aside for an hour. Do not move the slide. Now view the yeast culture again. Count the number of yeast cells. How fast does budding occur?

GROWING BACTERIAL CULTURES

Bacteria are such tiny plants that to see them with the naked eye one grows them in large numbers called colonies. They often appear as white patches. Bacteria will grow only if they have the right kind of food. Agar is a good medium.

Everything used in this experiment, including the measuring spoon, should be sterilized by boiling in water for fifteen minutes.

Bring 1/2 cup of water to a boil. Stir in one teaspoon of powdered agar and boil for five minutes. (If you can't get agar, stir in 1/4 tablespoon of gelatin

Bacteria can be classified by three basic shapes:

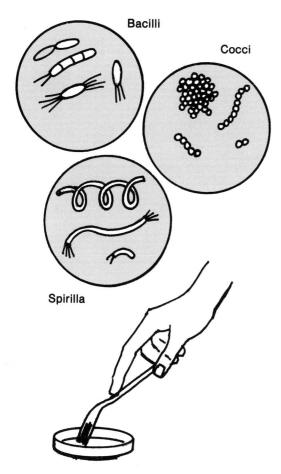

Bacilli

Cocci

Spirilla

but exposed to the air for half an hour. Cover all plates after contamination.

Place the plates in a warm place for two days. At the end of this time, one to several white spots should be visible. These are colonies of bacteria.

Repeat the experiment, but put contaminated plates in a cold place for two days. How well do bacteria grow in a cold place?

After completing your study, boil contaminated dishes and cultures in water for one hour to kill any pathogenic organisms you may have grown.

and add 1/2 bouillon cube.) Pour a thin layer of the liquid in each of several flat dishes, such as petri dishes. Immediately cover each petri dish. The liquid will harden as the medium cools.

Set one aside as a control experiment. Do not even permit air to fall on this one.

Now contaminate the other plates with bacteria. Roll a pencil over one. Rub a dirty finger over one plate and the same finger washed with soap and water over another. Roll a soiled fork over a plate. Leave one dish untouched

DEFINITIONS

agar — culture medium made from a jelly-like substance found in red algae.

bacteria—any of numerous one-celled plants visible only by microscope; classified by 3 basic shapes.

colonies — mass of bacteria on a culture medium.

contaminate — to make impure.

control experiment — a scientific test to check the results of the other tests.

medium — in biology, a sterilized substance (as agar) used to grow bacteria, viruses, etc..

pathogenic organism — disease producing organism.

petri dish—a circular low, flat glass dish consisting of 2 parts that fit together like the top and bottom of a box.

sterilize — to destroy bacteria or other microorganism by means of heat.

GROWING THE LIFE CYCLE OF A MOSS

Take a hike into the woods to gather moss. It will usually be found in moist, shady places. Transfer the plants and soil to a woodland terrarium. Water well and do not keep your moss house in direct sunlight. A little sulfur sprinkled in the soil will prevent growth of mold.

Examine the tops of the little upright shoots with a hand lens. One kind will produce the sperm and another will form the eggs. After an egg is fertilized by the sperm a little stalk grows up out of the female plant. At the top of the stalk will be the capsule containing the spores. When the capsule breaks open the spores fall to the soil and germinate into new plants. The tiny green plants are the sexual generation while the brownish stalk and capsule are the asexual generation.

DEFINITIONS

asexual — a single mass of protoplasm that can produce another cell or organism; sporing is a type of asexual reproduction.

egg — a female gamete or sex cell.

germinate — to begin to develop into a new individual from a seed, spore, bulb, or similar organ.

sperm — a mature male gamete or sex cell.

spore — an asexual reproductive cell usually single and haploid.

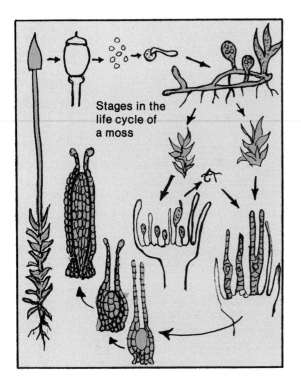

Stages in the life cycle of a moss

COLLECTING FUNGI

Fungi are found almost everywhere and are most successfully collected in the spring or fall months. Look for mushrooms, tree brackets, puffballs, toadstools, morels, lichens, smuts, molds, rusts, and mildew. Some grow on trees and bushes, some on riverbanks, in open fields, and still others on dead logs. Dry fungi may be put in jars or boxes. Fleshy fungi should be dried and placed in alcohol.

A living fungus collection may be raised in a terrarium—half woodland and half bog environment. The fungi grow best in warm, damp places. It is

Fungi come in many shapes

necessary to use care in digging them up from their natural habitat. Take a clump of soil and vegetation with their underground parts. Many fungi have rootlike structures called rhizoids or mycelium that may break. Keep the terrarium out of direct sunlight and water it often.

DEFINITIONS

fungi — plants that lack chlorophyll; group includes molds, rusts, mildews, smuts, and mushrooms.

MAKING SPORE PRINTS

Mushrooms reproduce by spores. One of the methods used in mushroom identification is making spore prints. A variety of specimens may be collected from damp wooded areas or marshy regions.

Remove the stipe or stalk from each mushroom. Spread a film of oil over a piece of cardboard. Rest the pileus, or cap, of the mushroom on two pencils over the cardboard. Put a plastic dish over this. Spores will fall and stick to the oil. Use contrasting colors of cardboard depending upon spore color.

DEFINITIONS

reproduce — to make a new living organism by a member or by members usually of the same species; may be sexual, requiring two masses of protoplasm, or asexual, involving only one mass of protoplasm.

spore — an asexual reproductive cell, usually single and haploid.

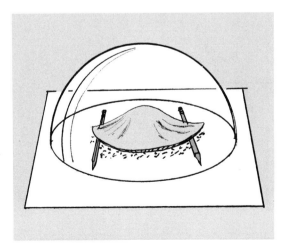

PREVENTING THE GROWTH OF BACTERIA

Why do pickles, jams, and bacon take a long time to spoil? They often use a preservative. Try the following to see how preservatives work.

Mix two bouillon cubes with a pint of hot water. Partly fill four clean glasses with the bouillon stock. Add one teaspoon of salt to one glass, one teaspoon of sugar to one, three teaspoons of vinegar to one, and nothing to the last glass. Put all four glasses in the same warm place. Look at them after two days. If the solutions are cloudy this indicates that there are bacteria and other microbes growing in it. Which additive acts as the best preservative?

What other ways can be used to prevent or slow down the speed of bacterial growth? As you walk through a grocery store list the various methods used to keep these from spoiling: canned tomatoes, milk, corn flakes, sticks of jerky, and hamburger.

GROWING A GARDEN OF MOLDS

Molds, a colorful group of fungi, can be grown on a variety of organic materials. They must be grown in covered jars since the host begins to smell bad as the mold feeds upon it.

Expose two slices of bread (one homemade and the other commercial) to the air for an hour. Mold spores will fall upon the bread from the air. (A quicker method is to wipe up a dusty floor with the bread.) Sprinkle each slice lightly with water and place each one in a covered jar. Put the jars in a warm, dark cupboard for a week. Bread

---

DEFINITIONS

bacteria—any of the numerous one-celled plants visible only by microscope, classified by three basic shapes.

additive — a substance added in small amounts to another substance to produce some improvements in properties.

microbe — a germ or bacterium particularly one causing disease.

preservative — any natural or man-made chemical that is added to a second substance to slow down decaying or spoiling.

mold has white stalks with little black balls on the ends. These are the spore cases. Which kind of bread molded faster and better? Preservatives are put into commercial bread.

Water mold can be made by placing dead flies in a jar of water. In a few days the insects are covered with a white fuzz. This is mold. Sometimes mold will attack fish in the aquarium.

An orange, apple, or other fruit that has been bruised can be bottled. The mold and bacteria working on the fruit gradually cause the cells to disintegrate.

Take four slices of the same kind of bread and leave them in the open air for one hour. Sprinkle each slice with the same amount of water. Place in separate covered jars. Put one jar in a warm, dark cupboard. Keep a second jar in the refrigerator. A third jar goes in a cupboard without its cover. Place the fourth jar in the sunlight. Leave all the containers in place for the same length of time. Compare the growth of mold after several days. Does mold grow faster in a warm or cold temperature, in light or dark, under wet or dry conditions?

DEFINITIONS

cell — the basic unit of living matter.

disintegrate — break into parts.

fungi — plants that lack chlorophyll; group includes molds, rusts, mildews, smuts, and mushrooms.

host — a plant or animal that provides food, shelter, or other living conditions for a parasite.

molds — any of numerous fungi which form either masses of dense, downy, threadlike growths or slimy growths on vegetable and animal matter; often produce decay.

organic — pertaining to, derived from, or composed of, living organisms.

preservative — any natural or man-made chemical that is added to a second substance to slow down decaying or spoiling.

spore — an asexual reproductive cell, usually single and haploid.

Chapter 2
Discovering the World of Higher Plants

STUDYING POLLEN

Cover a microscopic slide with a film of oil. Set it outside for several hours on a windy day in an area of blooming weeds and grasses. Pollen as well as other bits will stick to it. View them under a microscope.

How does the sperm fertilize the egg? Make a thin sugar solution. This will serve as a medium in which the pollen grains can grow. Locate a freshly-opened flower. Place the solution in a shallow dish and shake the stamens over the solution. Cover the dish and permit it to stand for an hour. Using a hand lens observe the long extension that has sprouted from each grain. This is the pollen tube. It grows down the style of the pistil until its nucleus joins the nucleus of the egg.

DEFINITIONS

egg — a female gamete or sex cell.

fertilize — to join egg and sperm nuclei.

medium — a food source for the growth of cells or organisms, especially bacteria.

nucleus — in biology, the mass of protoplasm in living cells which controls cellular activity.

pistil — the female floral organ, a structure in flowers, usually including the stigma, style, and ovary.

pollen — a fine dust, often yellow, produced and discharged by the stamens in a flower, and consisting of usually two cells which fertilize the nuclei of the female.

sperm — a mature male gamete or sex cell.

stamen — the male organ in a flower that produces pollen; usually includes anther and filament.

style — in flowers, the usually slender, elongated middle section of the pistil connecting stigma and ovary.

COUNTING THE PROBABILITY OF INCOMPLETE DOMINANCE

You can set up a simulation game to illustrate Mendel's work in genetics with garden peas. In 1865 he crossed red flowered peas with white flowered peas and came up with a ratio of colors that still holds true today.

Purchase a pound of kidney beans and a pound of navy beans. Be sure that you have 100 seeds of each color. Put the 200 seeds into one sack and shake well to mix them up. Reach into the sack, without looking, and select two seeds at a time. Record combinations until all 200 have been selected. Two kidney beans represent a flower that is homozygous for red. Two navy beans represent a flower that is homozygous for white. A red and white pair is heterozygous for red. Since red is not dominant over white these flowers are recorded as pink. What ratio did you come up with—the number of reds to whites to pinks?

What would happen if you crossed two pink flowers? Can you produce some flowers that are red and some that are white? Take the pile of seeds that were recorded as pink, put just those in a sack and repeat the selection procedure above. What can you conclude?

For additional information see page 83

DEFINITIONS

dominant — of a gene, expressing itself physically in preference to all others.

genetics — the science of heredity concerned with the transmission of physical traits in organisms.

heterozygous — an organism to which parents have contributed unlike genes for one or more inherited characters, although the organism may resemble one parent because of gene dominance.

homozygous — an organism whose parents contribute similar genes for some inherited character; having identical pairs of genes.

ratio — a proportion; the quotient of one physical measure divided by another of similar units; always a number with no dimension: a percentage is a ratio.

simulation — acting, looking, or assuming like something else.

EXTRACTING DYES FROM PLANTS

Natural dyes can be obtained from a variety of fruits and vegetables. Here are a few suggestions: light brown, yellow, and orange from onion skins, roots of white mulberry, wood from sumac, roots from osage orange hedge, and carrots; green from spinach; rose from beets, pokeweed berries, and roots from dogwood; gold from goldenrod flowers; brown from coffee and hulls of black walnut; red from red sumac berries, bloodroot roots, and red raspberries; black from red sumac leaves; blue from red maple and blue ash bark, and blueberries; purple from red cedar roots.

Chop the leaves, grind the roots, or crush the berries. Soak them overnight in enough water to cover. The next day boil them slowly for an hour. Strain the solution to remove all plant fibers. Add a little alum. You are now ready to dye material. Select white pieces of cotton, silk, rayon, nylon, or wool. Wet and wring out the pieces first in water. Put them in the dye bath. Be sure all pieces are completely covered. Simmer them slowly until the cloth is the desired color. When dry the material will be a little lighter.

If you use one quart of berries, roots or leaves, two quarts of water, and one ounce of alum, you can dye one fourth of a pound of fabric.

Once people dyed all their clothes by using natural plant pigments.

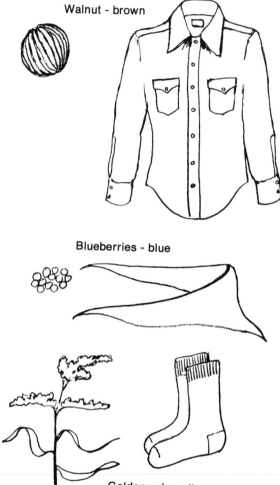

Walnut - brown

Blueberries - blue

Goldenrod - yellow

DEFINITIONS

alum — a crystalline material that has no odor or color; any aluminum sulfate double salt such as potassium aluminum sulfate.

pigment — a substance that gives color to the tissues of living organisms, as the green in leaves, the orange in carrots, and the red in beets.

GROWING FLOWERS FROM VEGETABLES

Select a variety of vegetables that store food in their roots, stems, or leaves. Many of these plants are biennials and do not produce flowers until the second year. You will be propagating from the first year's growth.

Cut the bottom half off such roots as a carrot, beet, turnip, radish, and sweet potato. Push the cut ends into a pot of wet sand or vermiculite. Underground stems such as the potato will root if half of it is submerged in a glass of water. Onion bulbs may be planted directly into a pot of rich garden soil. All of these vegetables will take root, send up new shoots, and soon a flower head will appear.

Leaf propagation can be done with a red cabbage. Cut the top half off and eat it. Set the bottom half in a dish of pebbles and water. It will sprout branches and a lovely reddish bush will grow. Peel away and discard the rotting leaves of the propagating plant as they die. Rotten cabbage has an unpleasant odor.

DEFINITIONS

biennial — a plant that needs two growing seasons to complete its life cycle from seed to seed.

propagating — bringing about production of an organism; in plants reproducing from the root, stem, or leaf of the parent plant.

vermiculite — a soft, light mineral; any one of the hydrous silicates which expands considerably when heated.

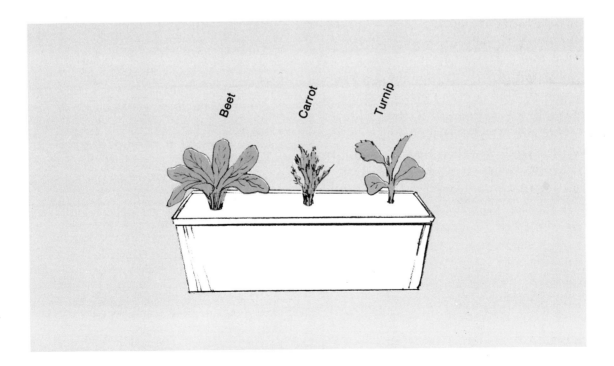

Chapter 3
Experimenting With Plant Processes

CALCULATING THE RATE OF SEED GERMINATION

Test the rate of germination with a variety of seeds, such as radish, corn, bean, apple, pumpkin, sunflower, and citrus fruit seeds. Soak the seeds for twenty-four hours to loosen their seed coats. Use at least three seeds of each kind since some will be defective and never germinate.

Collect a number of used paper cups (a way of recycling) and punch holes in the bottoms for good drainage. Fill the cups with sand or vermiculite. Plant all seeds at the same depth, about 1/2 inch under the surface. The amount of water, light, and heat should be kept uniform.

Observe your experiment daily. Which seeds sprouted first? Which ones took the longest? Record the date of germination for each kind. Once they are above the surface, measure the height of the growing stems daily. Which kind grows the quickest? How soon do the leaves appear? Following the experiment, transplant the young plants outside or in pots with loam rich in the nutrients necessary for healthy growth.

DEFINITIONS

defective — lacking something essential.

germination — the beginning of development into a new individual seed, spore, bulb, or similar organ.

loam — a fertile, rich soil composed of varying amounts of silt, clay, sand, and humus.

nutrient — a substance used by an organism for carrying on its cellular functions; a food.

vermiculite — a soft, light mineral; any one of the hydrous silicates which expands considerably when heated.

GROWING TREE SEEDS

Many seeds need the freezing conditions of winter to loosen their seed coats. The technique of stratification will simulate winter. Fill a tray with wet sand and bury the seeds in this mixture. Put the tray in a freezer for four to six weeks. One can speed up the germination of nuts, such as acorns, by drilling a tiny hole through the tough seed coat or shell. Be careful not to damage the seed and the embryo on the inside.

Collect seeds from a variety of trees—ash, maple, pine, oak, elm, and others. Plant the seeds several inches apart in a woodland terrarium or pots of rich garden soil. Keep them well watered.

The seeds with a thinner coat will germinate and grow faster. It takes time for the seed in an acorn to break through the thick coat and appear. As soon as the young saplings are several inches tall they may be planted outside. Put a wire cylinder around them the first year or two to prevent animals from stepping on them or chewing on the bark. Water and fertilize when needed.

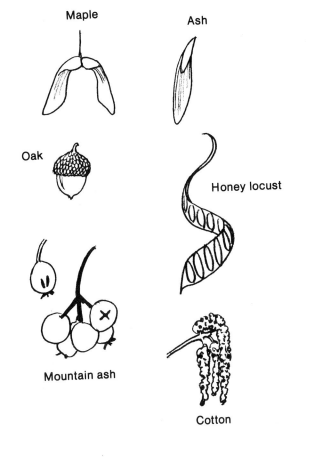

Maple

Ash

Oak

Honey locust

Mountain ash

Cotton

DEFINITIONS

germinate — to begin to develop into a new individual from a seed, spore, bulb, or similar source; to cause such a development to begin.

predict — to forecast coming events based on accurate observations and a systematic interpretation of the observations.

21

PROVIDING RAW MATERIALS FOR PHOTOSYNTHESIS

The chemical formula for the process of photosynthesis is $6CO_2 + 6H_2O + \text{light} + \text{chlorophyll} = C_6H_{12}O_6 + 6O_2$. The raw materials needed are carbon dioxide and water. Set up the following experiment to check this out.

Where can one get some CO_2? Secure a small jar with a cap and fill it half full of water. Add a teaspoon of baking soda. Let it bubble for a few seconds then cap it. When it is through reacting, uncap the jar and quickly insert a lighted match in the mouth of the jar. What happens? What gas puts out a fire?

Pour water into two test tubes. Put 1/4 teaspoon of baking soda in one. Cut two three-inch sprigs of Elodea under water, making sure you have the top end of the plant. Quickly insert a plant upside down into each tube. The end you cut is just under the water level at the top of the tube. Place a light over this set-up. With a partner time for one minute the number of bubbles leaving the cut ends of the Elodea in each container. Which one bubbled the most? Study the equation written above. Have you provided all the ingredients needed on the left hand side of the formula? What element was in the air bubbles coming out the cut ends? In which tube did you increase the rate of photosynthesis?

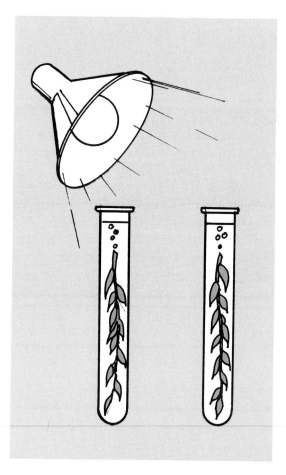

For additional information see page 83

DEFINITIONS

Elodea — an aquatic plant with green leaves and small flowers; also called Anacharis.

equation — a symbolic form for expressing a chemical reaction.

photosynthesis — the production, by green plants, of simple sugar from carbon dioxide and water, releasing oxygen and water; occurs in chloroplasts of green plant cells and in the presence of light.

TESTING GASES PLANTS GIVE OFF

Place a sprig of Elodea in each of two test tubes filled with water. Put a couple of inches of water into two short, wide-mouthed bottles, such as peanut butter jars. Place your finger over the open end of the tube and invert it into the jar of water without losing any of the water. Do the same with the other test tube.

Place one jar in a sunny place

Place one jar in a dark place

You now have two identical set-ups. Place one in a sunny window or under a grow lamp. Put the other one in a dark closet. After two days gas should have collected at the top (really the bottom) of the test tube by displacing some water.

Testing what gas was formed may be done with a lighted match. Put your finger or small cardboard over the open end of the tube that is under water. Invert it. Have a partner light a match and when you remove the cardboard quickly hold the match over the open end of the tube while the gas is escaping. Does the match burn brighter or does it go out? What gas does a green plant use in the sunlight and what gas is given off in the process of photosynthesis? At night the plant is carrying on respiration. What gas is given off then?

For additional information see page 83

DEFINITIONS

photosynthesis — the production, by green plants, of simple sugar from carbon dioxide and water, releasing oxygen and water; occurs in chloroplasts of green plant cells and in the presence of light.

respiration — in living cells, the breaking apart of food, such as sugar, into carbon dioxide and water with the release of energy necessary for cell activities; the opposite of photosynthesis.

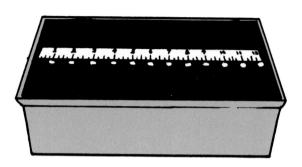

SHOWING THE STRENGTH OF GROWING SEEDS

The number of seeds needed for this experiment depends upon the size of the plastic container. It must be full to the brim. Pour water over the seeds and let them soak for twenty-four hours. Pour off the water, put on the cover, and tape it securely in several places. Keep the container in a warm place for several days. What happens? Does this help explain how rocks and sidewalks are often broken by growing plants?

Weigh twelve bean seeds. Weigh a twelve-inch ruler. What is the ratio in ounces? Plant a row of seeds one inch apart in a long tray. Cover with 1/2 inch of soil and water well. Lay the ruler directly on the row of planted seeds. As the seeds germinate can they lift the ruler? Would fewer seeds do the same job? Try corn, peas, and radish seeds. Predict the results before each experiment. How close did you come to guessing the strength of growing plants?

DETERMINING THE ROLE OF CHLOROPHYLL

Obtain a leaf from a coleus plant that has been in sun for at least a day. It is particularly good for this experiment since the pigments vary from green, maroon, and pink to white. Draw the leaf and label the colors in their appropriate positions.

Put the leaf in boiling water for one minute to break down the cell walls and bleach out some of the pigments. Remove the leaf and place it in hot alcohol for several minutes. (**CAUTION:** *Heat the alcohol on a hot plate—never over an open flame.*) The alcohol will remove most of the chlorophyll. Carefully rinse the leaf in tap water and spread it out in a flat dish. Add iodine solution until the entire bleached leaf is covered. After a minute rinse off the iodine. Which areas have turned blue or black? Iodine is a test for starch. Which areas are brown, the iodine color? Compare your end product with your original drawing and draw conclusions.

For further information see page 84

DEFINITIONS

chlorophyll — a green pigment in plants that is the site for the manufacture of sugar.

iodine — a heavy, grayish solid chemical element in the halogen family; readily gives off a purplish vapor; poisonous and corrosive; used in medicines, dyes and for making organic compounds.

pigment — a substance that gives color to the tissues of living organisms, as the green in leaves, the orange in carrots, and the red in beets.

starch — a complex carbohydrate, the main food storage substance in plants; derived chiefly from wheat, potatoes, corn, and rice.

DETERMINING HOW MUCH SOIL PLANTS USE

Weigh the amount of dry soil necessary to fill a flower pot. Weigh three seeds. Record amounts. Plant the seeds in the potting soil and water. Permit them to grow until they are several inches tall. Remove the plants making sure you have brushed all particles of soil from the root system back into the pot. Spread the soil out on newspaper until it is thoroughly dry. Now reweigh the soil. Weigh the plants. Compare these weights with your original figures. How can you account for the differences? Where did the extra mass come from? Would this hold true if you were experimenting with animal weight instead of plants?

For additional information see page 84

replanting. Seal the hole around the stem with soft paraffin so that it is airtight. Screw the jar down into the lid.

Keep the plant in a dark place overnight. Unscrew the jar and very quickly drop a lighted match into the jar. It will go out immediately, indicating that oxygen has been used up and carbon dioxide produced inside the jar. The carbon dioxide was given off in the process of respiration. Why must the plant be kept in the dark?

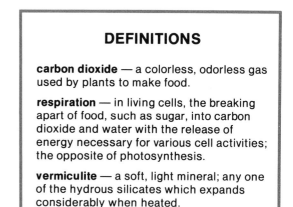

DEFINITIONS

carbon dioxide — a colorless, odorless gas used by plants to make food.

respiration — in living cells, the breaking apart of food, such as sugar, into carbon dioxide and water with the release of energy necessary for various cell activities; the opposite of photosynthesis.

vermiculite — a soft, light mineral; any one of the hydrous silicates which expands considerably when heated.

FINDING OUT THAT PLANTS BREATHE

Grow a plant from a seed in a large flower pot filled with vermiculite. When it is a few inches tall, dig it up carefully so that you don't break the roots. Punch a hole in the lid of a jar large enough to pass the roots through. The roots should go through from the inside to the outside of the lid. Replant the roots in the flower pot with soil so that the jar lid is upside down. Water the plant after

GETTING RAW MATERIAL INTO A PLANT

Plants need to get air into their bodies in order to carry on photosynthesis. There are tiny pores or stoma that let the air in. What compound is necessary besides water to make sugar?

Keep a plant in the dark for several days. A geranium works well for this experiment. At the end of this time do the following to three leaves. Do not remove the leaves from the plant. Coat the entire upper surface of one leaf with petroleum jelly or grease of some sort. Coat the lower surface of a second leaf. Coat both the upper and lower surfaces of a third leaf. The plant should be set in front of a sunny window for a week. Check the results. Have any of the three leaves died or are turning brown? Where are the holes or stoma on a leaf?

For additional information see page 84

DEFINITIONS

photosynthesis — the production, by green plants, of simple sugar from carbon dioxide and water, releasing oxygen and water; occurs only in chloroplasts of green plant cells and in the presence of light.

stoma — a tiny opening, usually on the lower surface of a leaf, which lets in carbon dioxide for photosynthesis and lets water out during transpiration.

OBSERVING TRANSPIRATION

Tie a clear plastic bag over the leaves and stem of a plant. Be sure none of the plant touches the bag except where it is tied securely around the stem just above the soil level. Set it in the sun for several hours. Observe what happens in the bag. Where does the water come from? A large tree will lose gallons of water a day. A plant that runs out of water in the soil will transpire itself to death. What factors can you control to reduce the rate at which a plant will lose water?

For additional information see page 84

DEFINITIONS

transpiration — the evaporation and loss of water from aerial parts of plants, especially leaves, through the stomata.

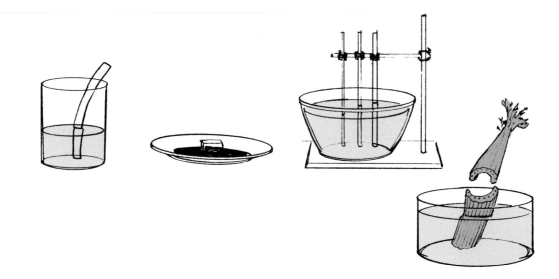

EXPERIMENTING WITH CAPILLARITY AND WATER COHESION

Put an inch of water colored with vegetable dye in a bottle. Place one end of a strip of blotting paper in the water with the other end hanging out of the mouth of the bottle. Notice the movement of water.

Set a cube of sugar or a mound of salt in a saucer. Pour in a film of ink solution. What happens?

Study an alcohol lamp closely. Notice that the upper part of the wick is not down in the bottle of liquid. Light the wick. What is burning? How did it get up to the top?

Set the ends of several glass tubes with varying widths in a colored solution. Does the liquid rise to the same height in all tubes? Explain.

Place a stalk of fresh celery in a glass of red dye. After one hour cut a cross-section of the celery and notice the red circles.

Water molecules adhere to the molecules of the material above it. This pull is greater than the cohesion or sticking together of one water molecule to the adjoining water molecule.

For additional information see page 84

DEFINITIONS

cohesion — the tendency for identical molecules to cling together; the force of cohesion results in the round shape of a water drop.

molecule — the smallest part of any substance that retains all the properties of the substance.

TESTING DIFFUSION

The molecules of liquids, gases, and solids are constantly moving around. Any solid that will dissolve in a liquid is soon spread by diffusion.

Set an open bottle of perfume or vanilla extract in one part of a room. Go to the other corner and wait until you can detect the odor. How did it get to you?

Put a few drops of different liquids (iodine, ink, vegetable dye) into glasses half full of water. Do not stir the solutions. What happens to the color of the water?

Place several glasses of water on a table where they may remain for two days without being moved. Put a cube of sugar in one, a piece of rock salt in another, a crystal of potassium dichromate in a third, and a ball of hard candy in the last. Do not stir them. What happens to each material?

For additional information see page 84

DEFINITIONS

diffusion — the movement of molecules of one substance into another substance; takes place rapidly in gases, more slowly in liquids, and extremely slow in solids.

potassium dichromate — a soluble salt forming large orange-red crystals used especially in dyeing.

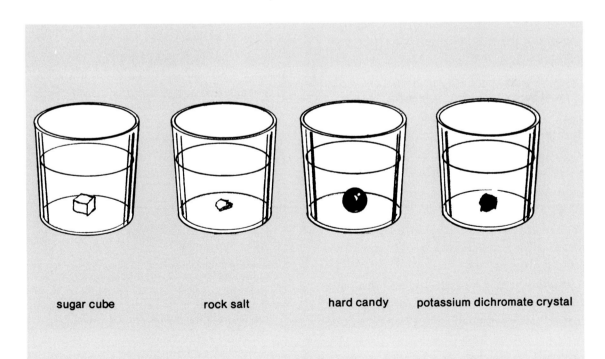

sugar cube   rock salt   hard candy   potassium dichromate crystal

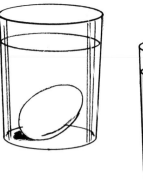
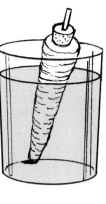

OBSERVING OSMOSIS

When two solutions are separated by a thin membrane, the more dilute solution will pass through it and move into the more concentrated solution if the membrane is permeable to it. Set up several osmometers, following directions below, to determine which solutions go in each direction.

Carefully remove part of the shell at the large end of a hard-boiled egg. Do not break the membrane under the shell. Immerse the egg in a glass of water. What happens?

Hollow out the top end of a carrot or beet. Insert a one-holed cork into the hollow and put melted wax around it to seal it closely to the root. Carefully put a glass tube into the cork. Be sure it is a tight fit; if not seal the cork with wax. Now place the carrot or beet in water that is colored with vegetable dye. Observe over a period of hours and draw conclusions.

Fasten a piece of sausage or hot dog casing over the end of a small plastic funnel with a thread or rubber band. Be sure it is tied tightly and that there are no holes in the casing that will serve as the osmotic membrane. Fill the funnel half full of a solution of molasses and water. Mark the level on the side of the funnel. Set the funnel in a jar with an opening small enough to hold the funnel up away from the bottom. Fill the jar nearly full with tap water. Observe every hour for a day. Which way does the liquid move?

For further information see page 85

DEFINITIONS

concentrated — containing a relatively high proportion of solute to solvent; said of a solution.

dilute — reduce in concentration; usually applied to solutions in liquids.

membrane — a thin layer of organic tissue which lines or surrounds organs and connects parts and has numerous other functions in all living organisms.

osmometer — an apparatus for measuring osmotic pressure.

osmosis — the movement through a semi-permeable membrane of liquids having differing concentrations of solute; this movement continues until the solutions on both sides of the membrane are equal.

permeable — having openings or pores that allow liquids or gases to pass though.

GROWING PLANTS WITH CHEMICALS

Make solution A by dissolving 2 teaspoons of calcium nitrate, 1/2 tsp. of potassium acid phosphate, 1-1/4 tsp. of Epsom salts, and 1/4 tsp. of ammonium sulfate into one cup of water. Pour this solution into 2-1/2 gallons of distilled water.

Make solution B by dissolving 1/8 teaspoon of each of these materials into a cup of water: zinc sulfate, manganese sulfate, and boric acid.

Make solution C by dissolving 1/8 teaspoon of ferrous sulfate into a cup of water. Add one teaspoon of solution B and 3 tablespoons of solution C to solution A.

Secure a large aquarium or similar container. Take a piece of wire mesh the same width, but several inches longer than the inside dimensions of the aquarium. Bend the ends and insert it so it forms a table a few inches above the floor of the container.

Pour in the mixture prepared above to the level of the wire. Scatter sphagnum moss over the wire table. This serves only to hold the seeds. Place the corn and bean seeds all over the top of the moss. The seeds will germinate, roots growing down into the solution. Continue to maintain the level of the solution throughout the growing period.

Experiment with other plants. Can you get the fruit of a tomato plant to develop without soil? Hydroponics means gardening with chemicals rather than with soil.

DEFINITIONS

chemical — an element or compound, found in nature or man-made.

DISCOVERING HOW PLANTS REACT

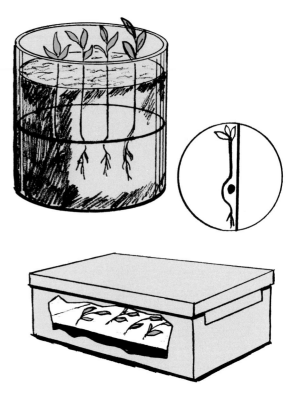

Unlike most animals, plants have only limited movement. They react toward their environment when different parts of the plants turn toward or away from a stimulus. This stimulus can be light, water, gravity, touch, or chemicals. Try these experiments on plants to test their ability to move. Have patience—don't expect a reaction in minutes. Some tropisms take hours to be noticeable.

Plant some seeds of sweet pea, clematis, or garden peas in a clay pot or directly in the garden soil if it is spring. As the plant matures drive thin wooden stakes in the ground next to the stem of each plant. Observe the action of the stem or tendrils as they reach for the stake. This is called thigmotropism and is caused by a touch stimulus.

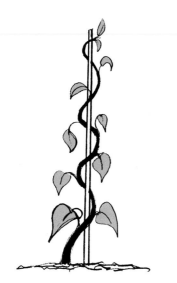

Line a shoe box with metal foil to make it waterproof. Cut the top two inches off one end of the box. Fill the bottom with a layer of gravel and cover this with good soil until the box is half full. Plant a variety of seeds. Water them well. Place the cover of the shoe box on and remove it only to water the young seedlings as they grow. After two weeks remove the cover and note the position of the tiny plants. Which direction are they leaning? What are they reaching for? This reaction is called phototropism or heliotropism.

Find an old aquarium or similar container for this experiment. Partly fill it with good soil. Plant seeds along the glass side at one end of the planter. At the opposite end bury a clay pot to within an inch of its top rim. Always water the plants by pouring the water into the flower pot and not on the soil at the end where the seeds are planted. Cover the sides of the planter with dark paper for several weeks. Then periodically observe the root growth of the seedlings. What are they turning for? This reaction is called hydrotropism.

Fill a jar half full of soil. Place a ring of copper wire around the inside of the jar so that it touches the glass. Finish filling with soil. Plant several seeds next to the glass. Cover the outside of the jar so that light cannot get in. Water the seeds well. Every week observe the roots growing straight down because of geotropism. What happens, though, when the tips of the roots are near the copper wire? This is called chemotropism.

Put a layer of cotton on a piece of glass. Place several seeds in a row across the center of the cotton. Corn, bean, and radish seeds will germinate quickly. Put a second piece of glass over the seeds and cotton, thus making a sandwich. Tie the glass together and set it on end in a pan of water. In two or three days the small seedlings will appear. In which direction are the roots growing? After the first week turn the glass sandwich around so the top edge is immersed in the water. Notice the roots are pointing up and the little stem downward. After a week in this new position, which part of the plant is growing down toward the center of the earth?

Make another glass sandwich as described above. Select one kind of seed, such as sunflower seeds. Place three seeds with the pointed end up, three seeds with the rounded end up, and three of them on their sides. Observe the direction of growth of each plant as it germinates. Can you see a pattern? Why does this occur? These reactions are called geotropisms.

For additional information see page 85

DEFINITIONS

chemotropism — growth movements of plants in response to chemicals.

environment — all the factors that affect either an organism or group of organisms; air, water, soil, climate, and other organisms make up the external environment, conditions within an organism make up the internal environment.

geotropism — growth movements of plants as they respond to gravity.

germinate — to begin to develop into a new individual from a seed, spore, bulb, or similar organ; to cause such a development to begin.

heliotropism — a growth movement of plants resulting in their turning toward or away from sunlight.

hydrotropism — growth movements of plants in response to water.

phototropism — growth movements of plants induced by a light stimulus.

stimulus — something in the outside environment that causes living cells to react.

thigmotropism — a growth movement in plants induced by response to touch or contact.

tropism — plant growth that causes a plant part to turn toward or away from an external stimulus, caused by plant hormones, usually auxins.

WATCHING MOVEMENT IN LIVING CELLS

An aquatic plant, Elodea or Anacharis, is the best for observing flowing protoplasm in cells. Select a tiny leaf from the tip of a sprig of this plant. The leaf is only two layers thick so the cellular structure can be seen clearly under the microscope. Place the leaf on a microscopic slide in a small drop of water. Do not put on a cover slip unless you are planning to view it under high power. Notice the chloroplastids moving around the cell walls. Can you find the nucleus? Now try the next experiment.

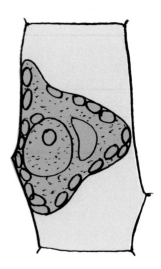

Enlarged view of Elodea cells with chloroplasts clumped in center.

CAUSING CELLS TO LOSE WATER

Take the prepared slide from the experiment at left and drop a few grains of salt on the leaf. Use the microscope again to observe the results. What happened to the chloroplastids? This process is called plasmolysis. Does this explain the damaging effects of salted streets in winter upon the vegetation along the roadside? Salt is used in food preservatives, in pickling, curing meat, and for killing tree stumps.

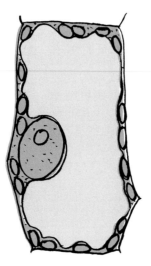

Enlarged view of Elodea cells with chloroplasts streaming around outer area near the cell wall.

DEFINITIONS

plasmolysis — shrinking of the protoplasm in a cell because of water loss through osmosis.

DISCOVERING THE AREAS OF MITOSIS IN STEMS AND ROOTS

Plant several corn or bean seeds in vermiculite. Do not plant in soil. When the seedlings are two inches tall dig one up and gently wash the clinging pieces of vermiculite from the root system. Be careful not to damage the tips of the roots. Blot the seedling dry with paper toweling.

Moisten thread with waterproof India ink. Holding the ends of the thread mark off the root into sections at one-eighth inch intervals. Continue up the stem until the entire seedling is marked. Wet a paper towel and lay it in a dish. Place the seedling on the towel with the marked side up. Cover the dish with plastic to prevent drying. Observe daily as the seedling continues to grow. Notice that the distances between some of the marks are getting wider. These are the areas containing the cells that are always dividing (mitosis). Which regions in a plant, whether it is a bean or oak tree, cause it to get taller and the roots to grow deeper in the ground?

For additional information see page 85

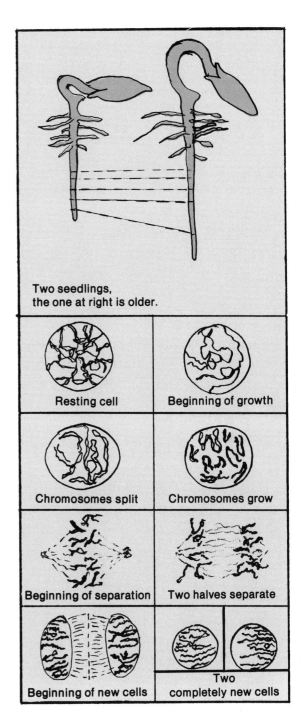

Two seedlings, the one at right is older.

Resting cell

Beginning of growth

Chromosomes split

Chromosomes grow

Beginning of separation

Two halves separate

Beginning of new cells

Two completely new cells

TESTING THE EFFECT OF HEAT AND LIGHT ON GERMINATION

Use one kind of seed for both experiments. You will test the effects of two different factors on germination: temperature and the amount of light. When testing it is important to keep all other variables constant except for the factor being tested.

Place a wet blotter or layer of damp absorbent cotton in the bottom of each of four dishes. Put a dozen seeds on top of each. Use two dishes for each of the two factors. One dish will be the experimental one while the other is the control.

In the temperature test, place one dish in a pan of ice water and the control dish in a sunny window.

Observe the rate of germination daily. What happens to each pair? Do seeds grow better in warm or cold places, in light or dark? Record your results.

For additional information see page 85

TESTING THE ACIDITY OF GROWING ROOTS

Germinate several seeds on moist cotton in a glass-covered dish. When the seedlings have grown good root systems you are ready to run the acidity test. Moisten several pieces of blue litmus paper with distilled water. Place the strips of paper beneath and on top of the rootlets. (**CAUTION:** *If the cotton in the germinator is too wet the test will not work.*) In two days observe the color of the litmus paper. Is it still blue? Knowing what acid does to rocks, does this explain how growing plants help break up the earth's surface?

DEFINITIONS

acidity — the state of a solution where there are more hydrogen ions than hydroxyl ions; expressed on a pH scale of 1 to 14 with 7 being neutral; the lower the pH the more acidic the solution.

distilled water — water that has the impurities taken out by the process of evaporation and then has the vapor condensed back to pure water.

germinate — to begin to develop into a new individual from a seed, spore, bulb, or similar organ; to cause such a development to begin.

litmus paper — a product made from the purple coloring found in certain lichens; used as an acid-base indicator, it turns red in acid and blue in base.

Place strips of blue litmus paper beneath and on top of rootlets.

Chapter 4
Doing Things in Nature

1 inch = 2.5 centimeters

MEASURING THE HEIGHT OF TREES

There are several techniques one can use to calculate the approximate height of trees, buildings, flagpoles, and other tall objects.

For the 11 to 1 method you will need a yardstick and a partner. Beginning at the base of the tree walk 11 paces in a straight line in one direction. Have your partner set the yardstick upright with the first inch at ground level. You will take one more pace, lie down on your abdomen, getting your eyes as close to the ground as possible at the end of the 12th pace. Sight past the yardstick to the topmost branch of the tree. This sighting, or line from the top of the tree to your eye, passes the yardstick at a particular point. Read that point in inches. For example, if the reading was 29 inches then the tree is about 29 feet high.

You will also need a partner, yard-stick, or long tape for the shadow method of determining height. This technique obviously must be done on a sunny day. You need to collect three measurements: your height, length of your shadow, and length of the shadow made by the tree. Use this ratio and a little math skill to figure out the unknown.

$$\frac{\text{length of tree's shadow}}{\text{length of your shadow}} = \frac{\text{height of tree}}{\text{height of you}}$$

The third technique is done by triangulation. Construct a triangle out of heavy cardboard. Holding the point at the lower end of the 45 degree slope next to your eye move away from the tree until you can sight the top of the highest branch at the opposite end of the slope. You will need a partner, standing to the side of you, to be sure you are keeping the base of the triangle parallel to the ground. When you have an accurate sighting, your partner should measure the distance from your

feet to the center of the tree's base. Now add this number to the height from the ground to your eye. This total will give you the approximate height of the tree.

Another technique is called the artist's method. Have a friend stand next to a tree. Hold a six-inch ruler upright in your outstretched hand. Let's assume your friend is five feet tall. Put your thumb on the ruler at five inches. Back away until the top of the ruler is at the top of his head and the five-inch mark is at his feet. Use this to measure the tree. Starting at the base of the trunk spot a place on the trunk that falls at the five-inch mark. Keep your eye on this spot and move the ruler up another five inches. You have now measured ten feet of a tree. Keep moving the ruler up, counting the number of five inches, until you reach the top. This is a rough estimate, but it is more reliable than a pure guess.

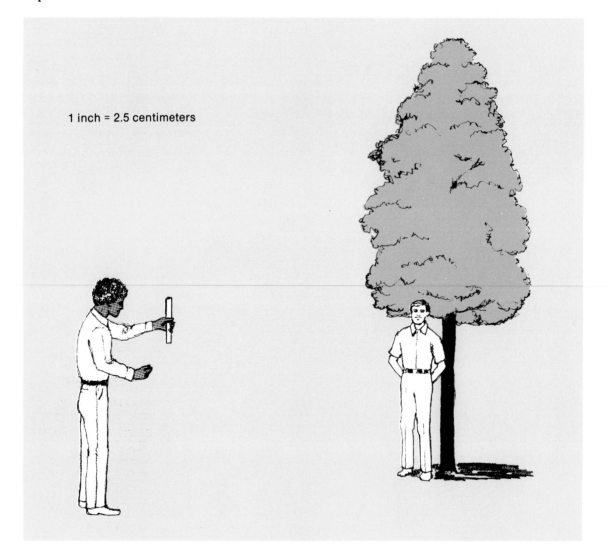

1 inch = 2.5 centimeters

STUDYING AN ECOSTRIP

An ecostrip is a long section (1 meter by 100 meters) through a community or ecosystem in nature. Select an area that provides a wide variety of plants, animals, and land formations. Mark off the strip with rope and stakes driven into the ground at the four corners.

If several people are involved in the study the following tasks can be divided to speed the process. It would take one person most of a day to do an effective analysis of the section. The diagram and data should be recorded on a large posterboard.

Identify all species of plants, their location and population count. Determine the height and circumference of any trees. Record which areas have full or partial sunlight.

Identify all species of animals. Take sweepings of the area with an insect net. Put specimens in jars for identification and number count at a later time. Examine the surface of the soil for any excrements, called scats, of higher animals. Take plaster castings of footprints left in the mud as animals passed through. Examine the soil for worms and other invertebrates. Look for animal homes, ant colonies, bird nests, and snake holes.

Do soil borings at different places, especially if the land includes a slope. Determine the gradation of the hill. Take the temperature of the soil at different locations and depths. Collect a sample of soil to be put through a soil sieve to determine the percent of clay, sand, gravel, silt, and humus. Test the pH and mineral count of soil.

Make a topographical map of the ecostrip. Identify any rocks in the area. Find evidences of any erosion.

Studying an ecostrip gives one a good picture of the nature of life and physical conditions in a total ecosystem. A stable community is a diversified one.

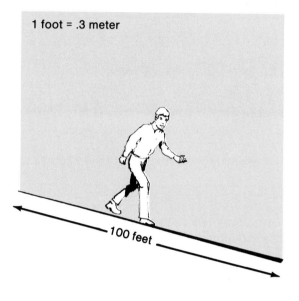

1 foot = .3 meter

100 feet

several times in order to provide a more accurate estimate. This technique of measuring only works well in an open, level area. Walking on slopes or through a woods will throw your pacing accuracy off.

DEFINITIONS

acre — a unit measure of an area, especially of land.

quadrat — commonly a rectangular area used for ecological or population studies.

DETERMINING YOUR PACE

A number of surveys or studies that one does in nature requires a fairly accurate estimate of an area. A quadrat, ecostrip, or an acre can be walked out if one knows one's pace.

A person tends to take a longer step with one leg than with the other, which accounts for going in circles when lost. Therefore, a pace is equal to two steps. Measure off a 100-foot distance on the sidewalk or hallway. Begin walking this distance with your left foot and count every time you put your right foot down. If you took 25 paces to walk 100 feet then your pace is 4 feet. Repeat this

PLANTING A VEGETABLE GARDEN

Plan to spend a good deal of time working on an outdoor garden. Things necessary for a successful garden are: good seeds, adequate fertilizer, periodic cultivation, weed control, and a well-prepared seedbed.

One must find a place for it that has sun most of the day and is close to a ready water supply. The first step is to test and condition the soil, adding whatever ingredients are needed for growth. Three primary foods required by growing plants are nitrogen, phosphorus, and potassium or potash. An inexpensive soiltest kit contains the chemicals and color chart necessary to run a test on the soil. Commercial fertilizer or your own homemade compost pile will help rebuild worn-out soil. Add this before cultivating to get the needed food at varying depths in the ground.

Be sure to buy healthy seeds or plants. To protect your seedlings against disease, root rot, and rodents, use a seed-protectant dust. Put a little of this powder in a jar with the seeds and shake gently till they are coated with dust.

Spade down six or eight inches in the garden area. Break up small lumps of soil and remove big lumps, stones, and sticks. Add the needed fertilizer and work it in. Finally, rake and smooth the soil level. Avoid tramping down the soil in the row areas.

Now plant the seeds or transplant the seedlings according to the directions on the package. Use string and stakes to mark off the rows. Allow thirty inches between rows for easy cultivation. As the plants grow they must be watered well at regular intervals if it does not rain. Never just sprinkle the garden; soak it well to encourage plants to grow a deep root system. Keep the soil loose around the plants and pull all weeds as they appear. They will sap the food and water supply from your growing plants. Watch for signs of disease and insect pests. You may need to spray with insecticide.

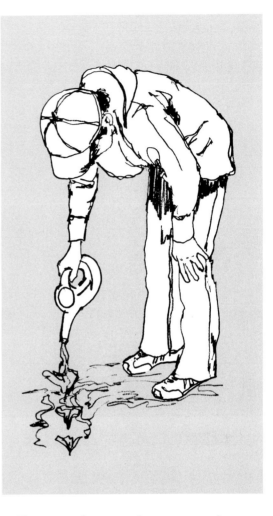

Do some research on organic gardening—growing plants without using commercial fertilizer, insecticides, fungicides, and other pesticides. What vegetables should be planted next to each other? For example, never plant beans and onions side by side. A row of marigolds will act as an insect repellent next to your tomatoes and cabbage. There is more to gardening than just throwing seeds in the ground.

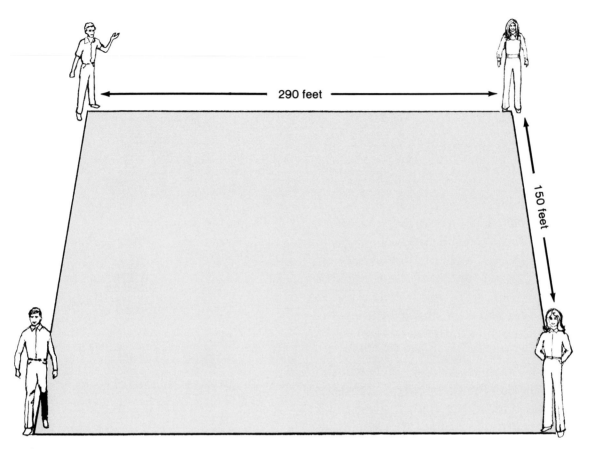

290 feet

150 feet

1 foot = .3 meter

WALKING OUT AN ACRE

Can you visualize an acre—43,560 square feet? Find three friends to help you. Using the pacing technique in the activity described on page 42, lay out an acre. One person will stand at the starting point. Three people will walk, counting your paces, 209 feet in one direction. One of the three will stand at this corner. The two remaining people will turn right at a 45 degree angle and pace another 209 feet. The last person makes another right turn and paces 209 feet. Each person is now standing on the corners of a square that outlines an acre. (An acre can also be a rectangle—436 feet by 100 feet or 290 feet by 150 feet.)

How big is the lot that your house is on? Pace the distance around the lot line and convert the feet into acres or a fraction of one. How many acres on the school grounds? Pace the length and width, multiply, and convert to acres.

USING BODY PARTS AS MEASURING DEVICES

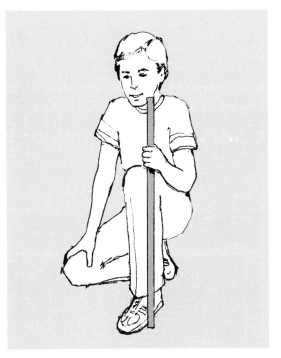

Before going on a trip to study nature it is helpful to make and record measurements of your own body. This will provide fairly accurate measurements of objects in nature, such as the height of shrubs and herbs, the length and width of leaves and flowers. It is wise to observe and record in the field. Leave nature as it grows rather than taking it with you. Leave the nuts and fruits for the wild animals. If everyone picked wild flowers they would soon become an endangered species or eventually extinct.

Here are suggestions for self measurements: length of index finger; length of hand from wrist to finger tips; length of arms outspread; length of foot or shoe; span between little finger and thumb tips when hand is expanded; height to knee cap, to the waist, to the shoulder, and to the top of your head.

Using your body parts as measuring devices will eliminate carrying a ruler, meter stick, or tape. Record the size and diagram the pattern of plants for identification later when you have access to books on trees, shrubs, wild flowers, fungi, and other lower plants.

Chapter 5
Working With Lower Animals—
The Invertebrates

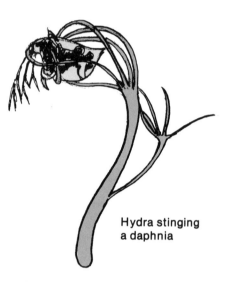

Hydra stinging
a daphnia

FEEDING A
STINGING HYDRA

These little freshwater animals may be collected from unpolluted ponds or streams or from a science supply house. Place the plants they are attached to with some of the pond water in a collecting jar. Transport them back to your room for experimentation.

Do not feed the hydra for two days so they will be very hungry. With an eyedropper, carefully suck up the hydra and place it on a glass slide. When it is relaxed and extended, gently place a daphnia (small crustacean or water flea) in front of its tentacles. Keep it moist. First the hydra will strike out with its tentacles, paralyzing the daphnia with numerous stinging cells. Then the tentacles wrap around the flea and bring it into the mouth.

There are other experiments to do with these fascinating animals. Shine a bright light on the hydra. When the hydra is fully extended, take a pencil and tap the end of its tentacles. Set the dish of hydras on an ice cube. Place the dish next to a warm bulb. What reactions do you observe?

DEFINITIONS

hydra — a tiny freshwater animal that has stinging cells on its tentacles and is composed of only two layers of cells.

46

FINDING ANIMALS IN A DROP OF WATER

One-celled animals are found in most fresh water, streams, ponds, lakes, or even a classroom aquarium. Take a large jar along when you go collecting. Fill the jar with an inch of mud from the bottom of the pond and then half full of pond water. Break off a handful of dried hay or grass growing along the bank. Add this to your culture.

Cook up about a dozen grains of rice. Add the rice to the culture. This will serve as additional food. Permit the jar to stand for one week undisturbed. Do not put it in direct sunlight. After a week put a drop of this protozoa culture on a slide and observe under a microscope. It will be teeming with one-celled animals, as well as minute water insects and flatworms. In a few weeks they will begin to die because of overpopulation and decomposition of dead animals.

DEFINITIONS

culture — the growth of cells or other organisms under carefully regulated conditions to avoid contamination.

protozoa — a phylum of one-celled animals and colonies made of like or similar cells; the most primitive animals.

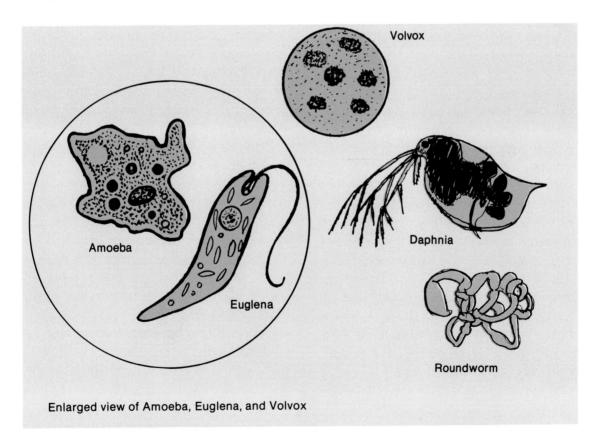

Enlarged view of Amoeba, Euglena, and Volvox

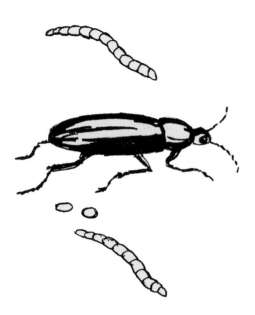

WATCHING "WORMS" GROW INTO BEETLES

Pet shops sell mealworms as food for pet frogs, toads, fish, and snakes. These "worms" are the larvae of little black beetles. The complete life cycle of beetles is seen in raising them.

Put several layers of uncooked bran or oatmeal in a glass jar. Sprinkle with water but do not make it soggy. Put in some pieces of raw apple or potato. This is food for the adult beetle. In several weeks the mealworms develop into beetles, the beetles lay eggs, and the eggs develop into mealworms. As long as the moist environment and proper food is maintained, the cycle of mealworm — beetle → egg → mealworm — continues indefinitely.

RAISING GENERATIONS OF FRUIT FLIES

Cut a piece of decayed apple or banana and place it in a glass jar. Put in a crumpled paper towel. Place a plastic or metal funnel in the mouth of the jar. After several fruit flies have been captured remove the funnel and cover the jar opening with a cloth. These flies seem to appear wherever fruit is decaying.

It takes about two weeks for the life cycle of the fruit fly. The adults lay eggs, the eggs develop into larvae, and the larvae mature into adults. The male has a darker band on the end of his abdomen. He has five visible segments on the abdomen, whereas the female has seven segments. The males also have ten black bristles (sex combs) on the tarsal joint of the foreleg.

In order to observe the sexes and to separate them into pairs it is necessary to put them to sleep for awhile. This can be done with an anesthetizer called "FlyNap" which must be purchased from science supply houses. It is not as explosive or as dangerous as ether, and it can be shipped by U.S. mail. Follow directions provided with the kit.

The flies may be poured out onto a white sheet of paper. With a hand lens pick a male and a female for each new culture. Write down the characteristics of each pair. Breed each pair in a separate jar, prepared as in the original jar. Observe and record each generation. Will two red-eyed parents always produce red-eyed offspring?

There are numerous chromosomal arrangements that occur in fruit flies enabling one to determine which genes are dominant, recessive, sex-linked, or lethal. Eye colors range from red, plum, white, apricot, eosin, and scarlet to brown. Body colors may be yellow, black, or ebony. Wings may be curly, dumpy, miniature, or normal. One is able to learn much about the laws of heredity by producing generations of these tiny insects.

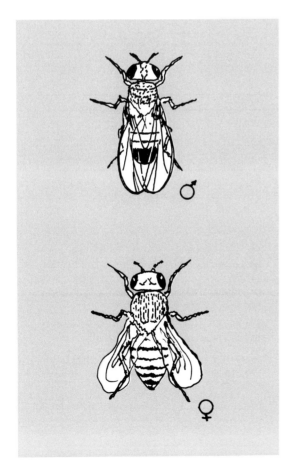

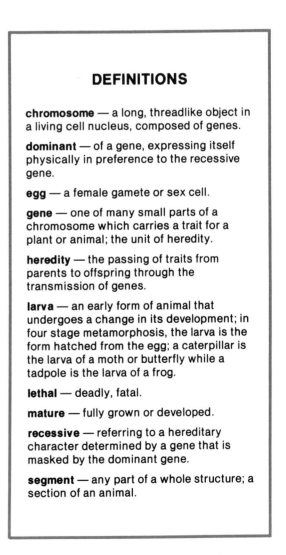

DEFINITIONS

chromosome — a long, threadlike object in a living cell nucleus, composed of genes.

dominant — of a gene, expressing itself physically in preference to the recessive gene.

egg — a female gamete or sex cell.

gene — one of many small parts of a chromosome which carries a trait for a plant or animal; the unit of heredity.

heredity — the passing of traits from parents to offspring through the transmission of genes.

larva — an early form of animal that undergoes a change in its development; in four stage metamorphosis, the larva is the form hatched from the egg; a caterpillar is the larva of a moth or butterfly while a tadpole is the larva of a frog.

lethal — deadly, fatal.

mature — fully grown or developed.

recessive — referring to a hereditary character determined by a gene that is masked by the dominant gene.

segment — any part of a whole structure; a section of an animal.

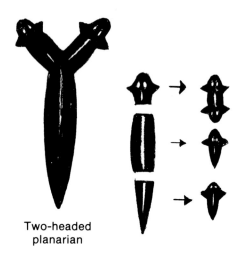

Two-headed
planarian

The planarian, a dark flatworm found in ponds or lakes, responds well to this process. With a small artist's brush transfer the flatworm from the collecting dish to a glass slide. Use a razor blade or sharp knife to do the cutting. If the animal is cut between the eyes to the middle of the body a two-headed planarian will regenerate in a week or so. Cut another worm the full length of the body. What if you cut a worm crosswise into three pieces? What if you cut it into five pieces? Which ones grew into whole animals? Does the anterior or posterior end have greater regenerative powers?

As animals increase in complexity they lose the power of regenerating large parts of their bodies. Can humans regenerate any parts of their bodies?

For additional information see page 86

REGENERATING ANIMALS

Regeneration is the growing on of missing parts. A starfish will grow an arm to replace a broken one or a crayfish will pull off a damaged claw and grow a new one. Regeneration is also a form of asexual reproduction. When a worm is cut in half, each half grows the other half.

Sponges also have great powers of regeneration. When a live sponge is pushed through a cloth mesh all the cells are separated. Soon they will clump together and grow back into a new sponge.

DEFINITIONS

anterior — toward the front or forward part of the body; contrast with posterior.

asexual reproduction — a single mass of protoplasm that can produce another cell or organism; fission, sporing, and budding are types of asexual reproduction.

complexity — the state or quality of being made of two or more parts.

posterior — toward the rear, farther back than other parts, used especially in anatomy.

regeneration — in biology, the growing of a new part to take the place of a lost or damaged one; the reproduction of a whole animal from a part of the parent stock.

FINDING OUT HOW
SNAILS BEHAVE

Snails are mollusks that carry their houses around on their backs. They glide along on a muscular foot that extends out the open end. Land snails can be found crawling over plants. Locate them in the evening or early morning when the ground and vegetation are damp.

Transfer the snails to a woodland terrarium containing damp peat moss and soil. Do not overcrowd. Observe their mode and direction of travel in the new habitat. They are usually more active at night. Use a strong light on the terrarium at night and during the daytime hours cover the container with dark paper or cloth. Can you reverse their behavior cycle (circadian rhythm) by simulating day and night?

How do snails react to gravity? Place an active snail in the center of a damp board which is propped up at a 45 degree angle. Which direction does the snail crawl? Tilt the board at various degrees until it is almost upright. What conclusions can you draw about a snail's behavior?

DEFINITIONS

circadian rhythm — a behavior pattern in plants and animals based on approximately twenty-four hour cycles; an inherited reaction to light, dark, temperature, or humidity.

gravity — the attraction or pull on objects toward the center of the earth.

habitat — the natural environment of a particular animal or plant; its address.

mollusk — a phylum of invertebrates with soft, unsegmented bodies (except for one order) covered by a fleshy mantle which usually secretes a shell; such as clam, snail, oyster, chiton.

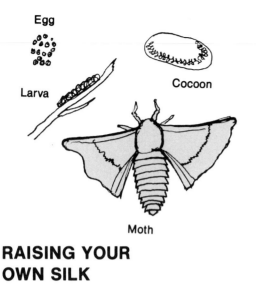

Egg

Larva

Cocoon

Moth

RAISING YOUR OWN SILK

Eggs of the silkworm moth are difficult to find in nature. Most biological supply houses will furnish them. Put the eggs in a glass-covered carton and keep them at room temperature out of direct sunlight. After a few days small black larvae will appear. Feed them fresh, dry mulberry or osage-orange leaves each day. In about five weeks put a stick in the box. The larvae will crawl on it and spin their cocoons. Drop the cocoon into boiling water for three minutes to kill the pupa. With great care unravel the silk fiber. A single fiber may measure three thousand yards.

DEFINITIONS

egg — a female gamete or sex cell.

larva — an early form of an animal that undergoes a change in its development; in four stage metamorphosis, the larva is the form hatched from the egg; a caterpillar is the larva of a moth or butterfly.

DESIGNING ANIMAL BEHAVIOR EXPERIMENTS

Construct a cardboard maze out of a suit or coat box. Tape sections of cardboard together to form a series of pathways with a number of dead ends and turns. Eventually a path should lead to the opposite end of the doorway. See illustration. Put a screen of wire mesh over the top of the box to keep your animal inside. Gerbils, hamsters, and white mice will react readily to this experiment. Select the animal's favorite food and place it at the far end. Set the animal inside the doorway to the maze. Observe and record the time it takes your pet to reach the food. Repeat the activity daily. How long does it take for your animal to become conditioned so that he heads for the food in the minimum amount of time and with the fewest dead-end routes?

Fish can be easily trained to come to a certain corner of the aquarium at feeding time. They will also take food from your fingers. This requires patience and placing your hand in the aquarium. In time the fish will become accustomed to the foreign object—your hand. They appear to enjoy being stroked as they adjust to the finger movement.

of factors and conditions to test the behavior of animals. (Remember: never involve an animal in an experiment that in any way harms it.) Animal behaviors can be classified as a reflex, instinct, insight, habituation, circadian rhythm, biological clock, conditioning, or imprinting. You may want to research these and design your own methods of testing out their validity.

Guinea pigs, rabbits, amphibians, and reptiles are good creatures to test food choices. Select a variety of vegetables, fruits, seeds, and meat products. Always do this experiment in the morning when the animal is apt to be hungry. The animal's balanced meal should be provided in the evening regardless of what experimental food was consumed earlier.

How do animals react to heat, cold, light, or dark? One can design a variety

DEFINITIONS

biological clock — the non-learned behaviors of living organisms that occur in cycles that may happen annually, monthly, seasonally, or daily; migration and hiberation are examples.

circadian rhythm — a behavior pattern in plants and animals based on approximately twenty-four-hour cycles; an inherited reaction to light, dark, temperature, or humidity.

conditioning — modifying so that an act or response previously associated with one stimulus becomes associated with another.

habituation — a learning process in animals where they no longer respond to stimuli if there is no reward or punishment.

imprinting — a form of learning during a very short period in the early life of an animal.

insight — a form of learning when an animal reasons out a solution to a new problem or situation; no trial and error period is involved.

instinct — an inborn response or reaction to a stimulus, a natural pattern of behavior that is not learned, such as a new-born animal that searches for food.

reflex — an involuntary response to a stimulus, frequently external.

validity — conforming to accepted principles of sound biological classification.

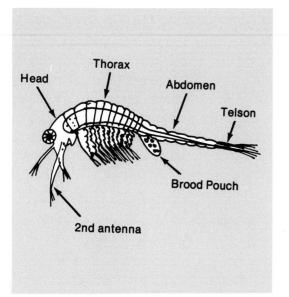

Head

Thorax

Abdomen

Telson

Brood Pouch

2nd antenna

RAISING BRINE SHRIMP

Brine shrimp are tiny animals that live in salt water. Eggs are often sold in pet shops that sell tropical fish. Dissolve fifty grams of non-iodized salt in a pint of distilled water. Permit the salt water to stand until it is room temperature, about 70°F (21°C). Place the eggs in the solution. In a couple of days the shrimp will hatch. Use an eyedropper to put a drop of the culture on a slide. With a hand lens or dissecting scope study their structure and mode of movement.

Chapter 6
Working With Higher Animals—
The Vertebrates

SETTING UP A FOOD CHAIN

The first link in any food chain must be a green plant since it is the only organism that can assemble a sugar molecule, the basis of food for non-green plants and all animals. A food chain is often illustrated like this:

Grass→cow→man or

algae→fish→bear.

Collect or purchase a culture of freshwater algae, such as chlamadomanus or euglena. Place the uncovered jar in the sunlight for several days until the population has increased to the extent that the water is bright green. These plants are the producers. It is now time to add the first level consumer, a dozen or so daphnia or water fleas. They will eat the algae, grow, and reproduce rapidly. When the food supply appears to be running out it is time to add the second level consumer, a dozen hydra. They will eat the daphnia. How can you keep your mini-habitat going until the energy flow comes to a halt? What freshwater animal could you add to keep the population of hydra under control?

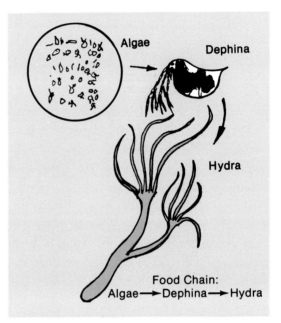

Food Chain:
Algae → Dephina → Hydra

The predator-prey relationships in nature are in delicate balance. Only fire, disease, and humans upset the equilibrium of food chains.

DEFINITIONS

equilibrium — a condition of stable rest or uniform motion resulting, not from absence of forces, but from the balancing of forces acting in different directions.

organism — an individual living plant or animal.

RAISING GUPPIES

Prepare an aquarium allowing at least a gallon of water for every pair of guppies. Supply ample plant life to provide adequate hiding places for the young. The mother guppy eats many things, including her offspring. Do not let the temperature fall below 70°F (21°C) nor exceed 100°F (38°C). Guppies thrive in warm water.

Guppies are live-bearers. When the female guppy is about to produce young, or is "gravid," place it in another aquarium immediately. It takes three to four weeks for a brood to appear after mating. Feed guppies commercial fish food, daphnia, or brine shrimp. Do not overfeed.

DEFINITIONS

gravid — pertaining to the condition of pregnancy.

brood — to produce by or as if by incubation: hatch.

FOLLOWING THE LIFE CYCLE OF A FROG

Gather a small gelatinous mass of frog eggs (no more than a dozen) from a pond in early spring. Place them in an aquarium with the same water you found them in. Soon tiny tadpoles will wiggle out. Separate them into several containers to avoid crowding. Feed the tadpoles bits of leafy vegetables and the yellow of a hard-boiled egg. Avoid overfeeding to prevent contamination of the water. Observe the tadpoles as they develop legs. Gradually the tails will be absorbed.

Construct a semiaquatic terrarium by placing a bowl of water in one end of an aquarium. On the other half build a land environment of sand, soil, and plants. When the tadpoles develop lungs they will leave the water habitat and seek the land. Adult frogs like living insects for food. Do not be impatient—it

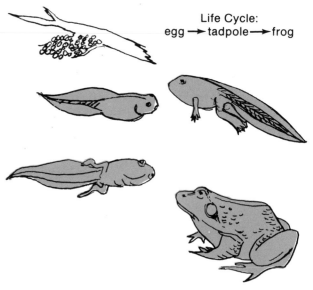

Life Cycle:
egg → tadpole → frog

may take a year or more with some species of frogs to go from egg to adult. Large bullfrogs take up to three years to complete this metamorphosis.

Day three   Day six

Day nine   Day twelve

Day fifteen   Day eighteen

Chickens hatch after 21 days.

DEFINITIONS

contamination — anything that makes impure (contaminates) something else; especially, waste material escaping into air.

habitat — the natural environment of a particular animal or plant; its address.

metamorphosis — the development of an organism after birth or hatching, involving changes in form and growth and usually accompanied by a change of environment.

WATCHING CHANGES IN CHICK EMBRYOS

Place two dozen fertile chicken eggs in a commercial or homemade incubator. Secure a bottle of rubbing alcohol to be used as a preservative for the embryos. Starting on the third day of incubation, break open an egg each day. Carefully remove the embryo and put it in a bottle of preservative. For the first five embryos dilute the alcohol with water by 50 percent. Dilute it by 15 percent, and then use it full strength for the older embryos. Continue the process for eighteen days. Observe the changes that occur in the embryonic development from egg to chick. Record the changes that happen daily, the formation of the head, legs, wings, eyes, beak, and other organs. Use a hand lens to see the details.

DEFINITIONS

embryo — in plants, that part of the seed that develops into the new plant; any organism in its developmental stages, before it has acquired the organs and functions necessary for independent existence.

incubator — a device for maintaining proper temperature so eggs can develop and hatch.

preservative — any natural or man-made chemical that is added to a second substance to slow down decaying or spoiling.

TESTING THE STRUCTURE OF BONE

Cook the legs of a chicken until the muscles and ligaments fall away from the bones. The bones will be whitish and hard from the minerals in them. Place one bone in a jar of water as a control. Put the second bone in a jar of vinegar. After several days to a week remove both bones. Are they still hard and brittle? Acid dissolves minerals and leaves only the animal matter. About two thirds of bone is hard mineral matter, most of which is calcium phosphate. The other one third is soft animal matter in the form of gelatin. What foods should you eat or drink to develop healthy strong bones?

DEFINITIONS

brittle — easily broken.

control — one set-up in an experiment where the variables are the same; it is used to verify a variable being tested.

ligament — a band of very tough tissue which connects bones to bones; may be fibrous or fold in membranes attaching organs.

mineral — a naturally occurring, inorganic substance with a definite chemical composition, characteristic crystalline structure, and distinctive chemical properties.

muscle — an organ composed of bundles of contracting fibers, held together by sheets of connective tissues, that produces movement in parts of a body.

Chapter 7
Learning About the Human Body

EXPERIMENTING WITH AN ENZYME

What happens to protein in the stomach? The cells in the wall of the stomach secrete a weak hydrochloric acid and an enzyme called pepsin.

Fill five test tubes 1/4 full of water. Place a small piece of cooked egg white into each one. Be sure all the pieces are the same size. Number the test tubes from 1 to 5 and add the following materials.

Test tube #1 — nothing else

Test tube #2 — 10 drops of 10% hydrochloric acid

Test tube #3 — 2 eyedroppers of 1% pepsin solution

Test tube #4 — 2 droppers of 1% pepsin and 10 drops of 10% hydrochloric acid

Test Tube #5 — same as in #4, but bring to a boil

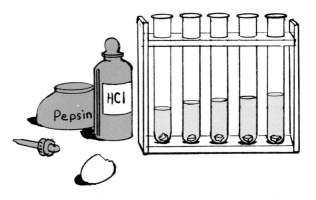

Set your five test tubes in a warm place. During digestion the temperature in your stomach is slightly over 100°F (37.8°C). After twenty-four hours observe any changes. The egg white will get digested in only one of the tubes. Can you explain why this happened?

For additional information see page 86

DEFINITIONS

digestion — the changing of food into a simpler form that an organism can absorb; usually done by adding water to a large molecule causing it to break into small ones.

enzyme — a protein molecule that speeds up a chemical reaction; it is not changed itself and can do it over and over again.

pepsin — a stomach enzyme that converts proteins into peptides.

protein — a group of complex organic compounds which is an important part of protoplasm.

secrete — to release a substance from cells in plants and animals for their own use.

TESTING FOR TASTE DISCRIMINATION

You will need a partner to help you discover things about your tongue. Your tongue is a receptor. It picks up taste sensations. However, as you will find out, taste differs on parts of your tongue.

Secure a number of applicator sticks. They can be Q-tips or toothpicks with a bit of cotton wrapped around one end. Prepare four solutions: sugar water; vinegar, grapefruit, lime, or lemon juice; salt water; and a concentrated solution of aspirin. A .001% quinine solution is also good for the bitter taste as well as the aspirin.

Start by rinsing your mouth out with water. Remember to do this after tasting each solution. Your partner will dip the applicator stick into one solution and touch all areas of the tongue until you can describe the taste. The tongue can be divided into the tip, back, center, and sides. Repeat this procedure with all four solutions. Diagram the tongue and record which areas picked up the taste sensations for sweet, sour, salty, or bitter.

Here is another test on the tongue which also involves another sense receptor, the nose.

Cut small cubes of raw potato, onion, apple, and pear. Take turns with a friend on this experiment and compare the results. The one being experimented upon should be blindfolded. Hold a piece of onion directly under your friend's nose and have him eat a piece of potato. Ask him which one he is eating. Repeat by smelling the pear and eating the apple. Which is more perceptive—the sense of smell or taste?

DEFINITIONS

perceptive — responsive to sensory stimulus; discerning.

receptor — any sensory nerve ending that receives information and passes it to the central nervous system.

DISCOVERING SOME FUNCTIONS OF THE SKIN

The lower or inside layer of the skin is composed of fat or adipose tissue. Try this experiment. It will help explain why fat animals aren't as cold outside in winter as those who are just "skin and bones."

Secure a cube of suet (fat) and a cube exactly the same size of lean meat. Leave them out of the refrigerator until they are room temperature. Check two thermometers for accuracy. Insert one thermometer into the cube of fat so the metal tip reaches the center. Push the second one into the cube of meat.

Set your experiment into a refrigerator or pack in ice. Check the temperatures every ten minutes. Which tissue, the fat or muscle, gets colder faster?

After an hour bring both thermometers and cubes out at room temperature. Which one warms up faster?

What would happen to the inside of the body if one had no skin? Select pairs of fruits and vegetables the same size for this experiment: two carrots, two potatoes, two oranges, etc. Remove the skin or peel from one of each pair. The second one is the control. Let them stand exposed to the air for a week or longer. What happened to the peeled specimen in color and weight? Explain. Have any fungi or bacteria attacked them?

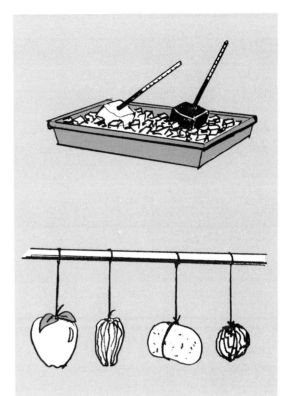

DEFINITIONS

adipose tissue — a specialized connective tissue that has animal fat stored within the cells.

bacteria—any numerous one-celled plants of division Schizophyta, visible only by microscope; classified by three shapes: coccus (spherical), bacillus (rod-shaped), and spirillum (spiral).

control — one set-up in an experiment where the variables are the same; it is used to verify a variable being tested.

fungi — plants that lack chlorophyll; group includes molds, rusts, mildews, smuts, and mushrooms.

For additional information see page 86

TESTING FOR CARBOHYDRATES

Place a few crumbs of an unsalted cracker (dietetic) in a test tube with about 10 ml. of water. Add ten drops of iodine and shake. If starch is present, the mixture will turn dark blue or black. Test a number of food products for the presence of starch. Why must starch be changed or digested before it can be passed out of the small intestine into the blood stream? Mix a teaspoon of starch in a cup of warm water. Mix a teaspoon of sugar in a cup of warm water. Which one dissolves?

Chew an unsalted cracker for several minutes. Has the taste of it changed? The enzyme amylase in the saliva has started to break the complex starch molecules into simple sugar molecules.

Now perform a more accurate test for sugar. Collect 3 ml. of saliva in a test tube. Add 3 ml. of water and a few cracker crumbs. Hold the test tube in your hand for ten minutes warming it to body temperature. Add 5 ml. of Benedicts solution to this mixture. Heat the test tube until it boils gently. If sugar is present, a red-orange precipitate will form.

A variety of foods may be tested for sugar. Partially cook several fruits and vegetables. Mash each separately. Add Benedicts solution and boil. Is there sugar in squash, sweet potato, apple, or lettuce?

Cheese

Meat

Peanut butter

Carrot

Egg slice

TESTING FOR PROTEINS

Proteins are important compounds in the cells all over your body. Knowing what foods are rich in these building blocks will help you select a diet that will keep you healthy.

Two solutions are necessary for this test. Make a 5 percent solution of copper sulfate. Make a second solution by dissolving a tablespoon of lime in a cup of water. Add equal parts of these two solutions to a slice of cheese with an eyedropper. If a violet color appears then protein is present. Try a variety of foods. Which ones have more proteins than others?

TESTING FOR VITAMIN C

Vitamin C or ascorbic acid is necessary for prevention of bleeding gums, for repairing damaged tissue, and for wounds to heal properly. It cannot be stored in the body, therefore one must consume this chemical regularly.

Make a vitamin C indicator by stirring a teaspoon of cornstarch into a cup of boiling water. Cool this mixture. Add drops of iodine slowly while stirring the solution. Keep adding until the mixture is blue. You are ready to test fruit juices, such as orange, grapefruit, lemon, tomato, and apple. Pour a small amount of the indicator into a test tube or drinking glass. Start adding drops of one juice until the blue color disappears. Record the number of drops it took. Repeat with each juice using fresh indicator each time. The more drops it takes, the less vitamin C is present.

Now try a variation. Boil a juice and test it. What did you find out? Let the juice stand for a couple of days in an open container. Test it for vitamin C. Compare your results on this test with your reading before. What happened? What does this tell you about the nature of this vitamin?

Add a little bicarbonate of soda to a juice and then test for the presence of vitamin C. Baking soda is often added to vegetables to preserve their green coloring. What happens to the amount of ascorbic acid under these conditions?

For additional information see page 86

EMULSIFYING FATS

Fats need to be broken down physically before the enzymes in the small intestine can break them down chemically. This experiment will show you how this is done. Materials may be purchased from a biological supply house.

Number three test tubes or bottles. Pour 9 ml. or 3 tablespoons of water into each container. Put 3 ml. or 1 tablespoon of a 5 percent bile solution into test tube number 1. Put 3 ml. of liquid fat (corn oil, melted butter) into test tube number 2. To number 3 add 3 ml. of fat and 3 ml. of bile solution. Shake each test tube while keeping your thumb over the open end of the tube. Allow all containers to stand for ten minutes. Describe the changes in each. What is the function of bile salts? How does having one's gall bladder removed affect one's diet?

For additional information see page 87

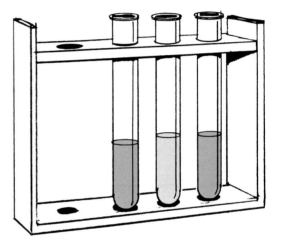

DEFINITIONS

bile — an orange or green fluid produced by the liver that flows into the intestine to aid in fat digestion; it is stored in the gall bladder.

emulsify — to break large drops of one liquid into tiny droplets which stay dispersed in another liquid.

fat — a material found in animal cells and seeds of many plants; any ester of glycerol with a fatty acid, used as an energy supply and for insulation.

TESTING CHEMICALS
IN EXHALED AIR

Fill a drinking glass half full with BTB solution (Bromothymol blue). What color is it? Put a soda straw into the glass and exhale slowly through it, bubbling your breath into the solution for a few minutes. What happens? Record. What is in exhaled air to cause this? Can you figure out how to get it back to its original color? What would happen if you put a sprig of Elodea into the BTB?

Now fill a glass half full with limewater. Put a soda straw into it and exhale slowly for several minutes. What happens to the limewater? The same compound in exhaled air caused this. Have you figured out what it is?

For additional information see page 87

CALCULATING YOUR
LUNG CAPACITY

Locate a glass gallon bottle. It will hold 4,000 ml. of water. You will need to mark a scale on the outside of the bottle with a grease pencil. Begin by pouring in 400 ml. of water at a time, marking the level with the correct figure. You will have ten sets of numbers by the time the bottle is filled. The water level marks will read from 400 ml. to 4,000 ml. with intervals of 400 ml.

Pour a couple of inches of water into a large dishpan or similar container. Have your partner put a hand over the mouth of the gallon bottle that has been filled to the 4,000 ml. mark. Quickly turn the bottle upside down with the opening under the water in the dishpan. The water will stay in the bottle. Have your partner insert one end of a two to three foot rubber or plastic tube several inches into the bottle. It is necessary to tilt the bottle slightly to feed the tube in and up.

You are now ready to check your lung capacity. Take a big deep breath and exhale it into the open end of the tube. Your exhaled breath will displace the water in the bottle. Your partner should then cover the mouth of the bottle and set it upright. Subtract the amount of water left in the gallon from 4,000 and that is the number of milliliters you breathed out.

Reverse roles and check your partner's lung capacity. Remember to dip the end of the tube you are using in your mouth into alcohol to disinfect it.

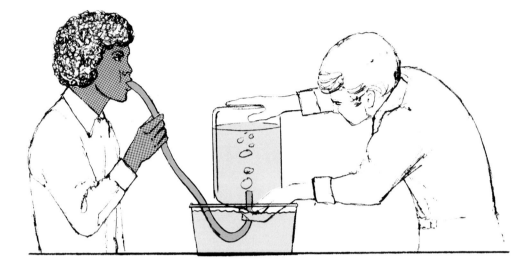

Daily exercise will increase your lung capacity. This is an important part of keeping fit and healthy. The muscles in your chest wall and diaphragm will contract and relax in a wider range with strenuous activity, thus making more room in your chest cavity for the lungs to fill with air.

One partner should serve as the test subject, the other will record and keep time. In all the following count one inhalation and one exhalation together as one breath. Allow at least a one-minute rest between tests or alternate partners.

Count the number of breaths per minute during normal breathing while sitting at rest. Record.

Take very deep breaths for one minute at a faster than normal rate. Now breathe normally and count the number of breaths per minute. Record.

Hold a paper bag tightly over your mouth and nose so that you are forced to rebreathe the same air. Do this for two minutes breathing as involuntarily as possible. During the second minute count the number of breaths. Record.

Stand up and run in place for one minute. Then sit quietly and count the number of breaths per minute. Record.

Explain the results in each experiment. Read about the respiratory center in the medulla, a part of your brain.

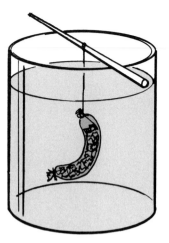

DEMONSTRATING ABSORPTION IN THE SMALL INTESTINE

What did you have for lunch today? This experiment will help you find out what happened to it.

Mash up small amounts of a variety of foods that you might eat. This could be bits of bread, peanut butter, grape jelly, apple, and milk. Add two eyedroppers of a 5 percent solution of pancreatin. Tie one end of a six-inch length of cellophane dialyzing tubing with thread or fine string. Pour the solution into the tubing. Tie off the open end. Your "meal" is now confined in a "small intestine." Wash off the outside of the tubing to remove any traces of the nutrients. Place the filled tubing into a warm water bath (40°C or 104°F) for twenty-four hours. The heat from a lighted 100 watt bulb will keep the temperature up.

You are now ready to run tests on the water that the tubing has been in. Use Benedicts solution for the carbohydrates test (see page 62). Use copper sulfate.

and lime solutions for the protein test (see page 63). Fats are digested into fatty acids and glycerol. Use litmus paper for this test. Blue litmus paper turns red in an acid solution. What enzymes are found in the pancreas?

For additional information see page 87

TESTING FOR FATS

A brown paper bag is all one needs for this test. Rub butter on a section of it. Does it leave a permanent grease spot? Try other foods such as a boiled egg white and yolk, peanut, apple, bread, hamburger, hot dog, etc. Wait until the water evaporates before you draw any conclusions. A wet brown bag is not a greasy one.

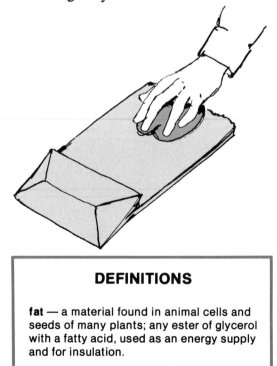

DEFINITIONS

fat — a material found in animal cells and seeds of many plants; any ester of glycerol with a fatty acid, used as an energy supply and for insulation.

as when your heart beats. A baby's heart beats over eighty times per minute while an old person's heart beats only sixty times.

The heart keeps about six quarts of blood flowing through your body every minute or two. That is a lot of work. The muscles in the heart rest for only a second between beats. How many times does the heart beat in an hour? In a day? A week? A month? A year? In a lifetime? Isn't the heart a marvelous machine?

For additional information see page 87

TESTING THE STRENGTH OF CARDIAC MUSCLE

Which do you think is stronger and tires less easily—the skeletal muscles in your hand or the cardiac muscles in your heart? Try this.

Squeeze a rubber ball in your hand around seventy times per minute. Keep squeezing and timing until you are too tired to do it anymore. Record the results. Each squeeze is about the same

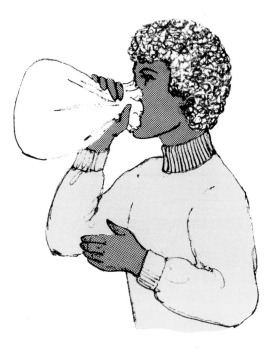

Count the number of breaths per minute during normal breathing while sitting at rest. Record.

Take very deep breaths for one minute at a faster than normal rate. Now breathe normally and count the number of breaths per minute. Record.

Hold a paper bag tightly over your mouth and nose so that you are forced to rebreathe the same air. Do this for two minutes breathing as involuntarily as possible. During the second minute count the number of breaths. Record.

Stand up and run in place for one minute. Then sit quietly and count the number of breaths per minute. Record.

Explain the results in each experiment. Read about the respiratory center in the medulla, a part of your brain.

MEASURING THE EFFECT OF CO_2 IN BLOOD ON BREATHING RATE

One partner should serve as the test subject, the other will record and keep time. In all the following count one inhalation and one exhalation together as one breath. Allow at least a one-minute rest between tests or alternate partners.

DEFINITIONS

medulla — the soft, marrowlike interior of bones and organs such as the kidneys and adrenals; the lower part of the brain at the upper end of the spinal cord.

TESTING YOUR EARS

Find a partner to help conduct these tests. The one being experimented upon (the subject) needs to block one ear with a wad of cotton or by pushing the inner lobe over the opening. The experimenter will hold a ticking watch in front of the opening of the opposite ear. Slowly back away from the subject until he tells you he can't hear it anymore. Measure the distance. Start farther away and slowly walk toward the subject until he hears the watch. Measure the distance. Repeat this activity on the other ear. What have you found out?

The subject will close off one ear with cotton. Strike a tuning fork on the rubber heel of your shoe. Hitting a hard surface will damage the fork. Place the end of the handle of the vibrating fork on the bone behind the subject's open ear. As soon as he says he cannot hear it bring the fork around in front, holding it so that you can see the ear between the U of the fork. Can your partner pick up the vibrations now? Can you draw any conclusions about sound traveling through solids or air?

Blindfold your partner or have him keep his eyes closed tightly. Use two metal spoons to make a tapping noise. Instruct the subject to indicate the direction of the sound. Tap the spoons together on his right side, left side, in front, in back, and above his head. Explain your results. Close off one ear of the subject and repeat. Does having two ears localize sounds for you?

For additional information see page 88

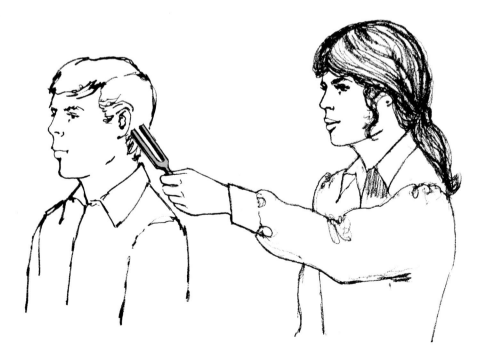

71

with alcohol. Hold the second clean slide (the spreader) on one end in the drop of blood at a 30 degree angle. Push the spreader slide the length of the first slide leaving a thin coat of blood. Permit the slide to air dry. Do not blow on it. It is now ready to be stained.

Put drops of Wrights Stain on the blood covering the whole smear. Let this stand for three minutes. Slowly add drops of distilled water until it equals the amount of stain. Let it stand for another three minutes. Hold the slide at an angle under slow running tap water until all surplus stain is washed away. As soon as the slide is air dried you are ready to view the blood cells under a microscope. An approximate ratio that is easy to remember is 800 red cells to 40 platelets to 1 white cell. Which cells are the largest? Smallest?

MAKING A FRESH BLOOD SMEAR

There are three types of cells in blood that one is able to identify under a fairly simple microscope. The red cells carry oxygen, the white cells fight bacteria, while the platelets help in clotting. One can prepare a slide of fresh blood and stain it so the cells can be distinguished from each other.

Wash your hands and two microscopic slides to remove the soil and grease. Shake your non-writing hand to get the blood into the fingertips. Sponge the tip of the middle index finger with 70 percent alcohol and permit the finger to dry. Puncture the tip with a sterile needle or lancet. Squeezing above the puncture, put a drop of blood on the end of one of the clean slides. Clean your wound again

DEFINITIONS

bacteria — any of numerous one-celled plants of division Schizophyta, visible only by microscope; classified by three shapes: coccus (spherical), bacillus (rod-shaped), and spirillum (spiral).

distilled water — water that has the impurities taken out by the process of evaporation and then has the vapor condensed back to pure water.

platelet — a minute cellular particle found in the blood of mammals, produced by certain large cells in the bone marrow; through fragmentation assists in clotting.

ratio — a proportion; the quotient of one physical measure divided by another of similar units; always a number with no dimension: a percentage is a ratio.

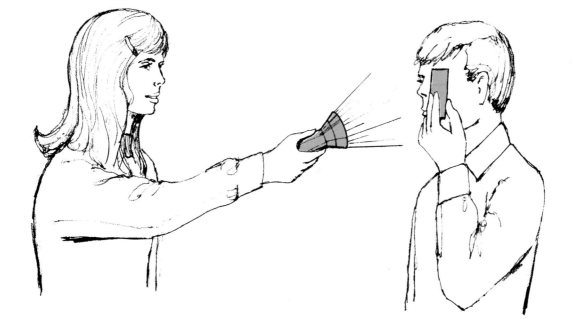

FIGURING OUT THE JOB OF THE IRIS

You will need a partner for these tests. You will be called the experimenter and your partner is the subject.

The pupil in the eye is the black hole in the center of the iris or colored ring. The iris controls the amount of light that will enter the pupil to reach the retina on the back part of the eyeball.

The experimenter looks into the eyes of the subject and notes the size of the pupils. The subject then closes his eyes and covers them with his hands. The experimenter shines a flashlight into the subject's face. At a given signal the subject opens his eyes. The experimenter watches the size of his pupils. This happens quickly so don't miss it.

Now the subject holds the edge of a heavy piece of cardboard against his face, separating the eyes. Be sure the nose is on one side of the cardboard. The experimenter will shine the flashlight on the right eye while watching the pupil of the left eye. Do the pupils adjust together or independently?

Does distance affect the way the iris contracts and relaxes? The experimenter should observe the subject's pupil as he or she looks at an object two feet in front of the eyes. Watch the pupils closely as the subject looks at an object on the other end of the room. Explain your results.

For additional information see page 88

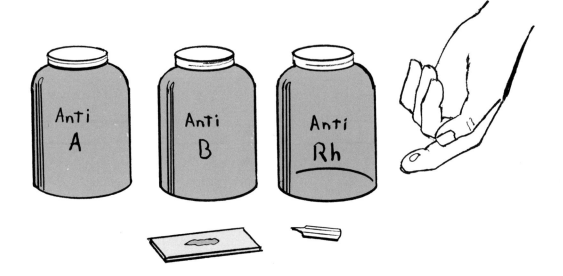

TYPING BLOOD

There are four major blood groups: A, B, AB, and O. A group is based on the presence or absence of antigens and antibodies. This is inherited. A person with A type blood has the A antigen on the red cells and the anti-B serum. Type B has the B antigen and anti-A serum. Type AB has both antigens and no antibodies. Type O has neither antigens and both antibodies.

This is how you find out what type you have in your circulatory system.

Purchase a small bottle of anti-A serum, anti-B serum, and sterile disposable blood lancets. In place of the lancet one may use a sterilized needle.

Wash your hands thoroughly with soap and water before beginning. Label two clean microscopic slides A and B. Shake your non-writing hand to get the blood into the fingertips. Sponge the tip of the middle index finger with alcohol and permit the finger to dry. Puncture the tip with needle or lancet. Squeezing above the puncture put a drop of blood on each slide. Clean the wound again with alcohol.

Put a drop of anti-A serum in the blood on slide number 1. Put a drop of anti-B serum in the blood on slide number 2. Mix the serum and blood on each slide with a clean toothpick. Examine the slides with the naked eye or with a hand lens for clumping or agglutination. If the blood on both slides clumps, it is type AB. If only the blood on slide number 1 clumps, it is A type. If slide number 2 clumps, it is B type. If neither slide shows clumping, it is type O.

It is necessary to know a person's blood type before he or she can be given a transfusion. In the United States type O is most common and AB is the rarest.

Another protein found in most people's blood is the Rh factor or antigen. To test for this one needs to purchase anti-Rh serum. Follow the procedure above for getting a drop of blood on a slide. Mix a drop of this serum in the blood. If it clumps you are Rh positive. Only around 15 percent lack this protein and are classified Rh negative.

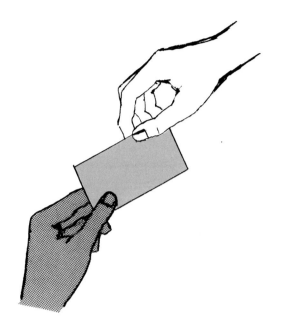

DEFINITIONS

agglutination — the clumping of particles, especially bacteria or blood cells.

antibody — a protein in blood serum that reacts with certain antigens in red cells that are introduced to the body, causing clumping.

antigens — any substance not normally present in the body which, when supplied, stimulates antibody production.

protein — any of a group of complex organic compounds which is an important part of protoplasm.

Rh factor — any of various substances (antigen), often present in human blood cells, that stimulate the production of antibodies; blood containing such substance is classified as Rh positive; blood lacking it, as Rh negative; an inherited characteristic, Rh positive being dominant.

serum — the light yellowish, watery part of the blood, containing antibodies.

transfusion — a process for transferring blood from one person to another, usually through a needle inserted in a vein.

TESTING YOUR REACTION TIME

Cut a piece of paper about the size of a dollar bill. Ask a friend to hold out his hand with his thumb and forefinger about an inch apart. Suspend the paper between them with your hand above his. Ask him to catch the paper as you drop it. Chances are he won't be able to close his fingers fast enough after he sees you let go. Experiment to find out whether your friend comes closer to catching the paper before or after eating, early in the morning or late at night, before or after strenuous physical exercise. Is a young person or an old person better at catching the falling paper?

STIMULATING YOUR REFLEXES

Simple reflex actions involve the organ receiving the stimulus, the spinal cord or brain, and a muscle or gland that responds. Check out your nervous responses with these simple tests.

Swing your hand quickly in front of a friend's face. Notice how fast the eyelids close. This is a protective reflex.

Have a friend sit on a chair with legs crossed. Strike the tendon just below the kneecap with the side of your hand. What happens to his lower leg? Have your friend hold tightly to the sides of the chair and attempt not to respond to your hitting his tendon. Can it be done? Have him clasp his hands in front of him and pull hard at the same time you are tapping. Does his lower leg move?

Salivation can be a reflex. Work your tongue and lips around as if you were chewing. When your mouth is filled with saliva swallow it. Put a few drops of vinegar in your mouth. What effect does this have on the glands that secrete saliva?

Hold your arms extended out to the sides. Swing them forward until your index fingers meet at the tips. Repeat this action with eyes closed.

Stand with your feet together and your arms outstretched. Repeat this with closed eyes. Have a friend watch what

happens to the position of your body. Stand on one foot and then the other while you are looking above you. Do the same thing but close your eyes. What happens? What conclusions can you draw about static equilibrium and your eyes?

Have someone tickle the back of your neck with a feather. Can you stop from having "goose bumps"? When you are embarrassed keep yourself from blushing. Don't permit the blood vessels to dilate in your face. As you get a strong impulse to sneeze, try to stop it. Do not touch your nose with your hand. All of these responses are reflexes.

For additional information see page 88

DEFINITIONS

dilate — to expand, as the pupil of the eye in darkness.

equilibrium — a condition of stable rest or uniform motion resulting not from absence of forces, but from the balancing of forces acting in different directions.

reflex — an involuntary response to a stimulus, frequently external.

saliva — a fluid secreted by mouth glands of vertebrates and containing in humans a digestive enzyme called amylase.

static — at rest; in equilibrium; pertaining to forces at rest rather than moving.

stimulus — a change in environment detected by a sense organ; may change behavior or start a reflex action.

tendon — a tough, fibrous, tissue band that connects muscle to bone.

LOCATING YOUR BLIND SPOT

On a small piece of cardboard or stiff paper draw a black circle about a half inch in diameter. Four inches to the right of the circle draw an X the same size. Hold the cardboard at arm's length and at eye level. Close your left eye or cover it. As you look at the circle slowly move the paper closer to your face. At a certain distance the X will disappear from sight. As you move the paper still closer the X reappears. Study a drawing of the parts of the human eye. What place in the back of the eyeball cannot pick up light rays? This is called the blind spot for it lacks rods and cones.

For additional information see page 88

CHARTING NERVE
ENDINGS IN THE SKIN

Find a partner to help explore the types of sensations you can pick up with your skin.

With a pen mark off a 1-1/4 inch (3 cm) square on the palm of your hand. Sub-divide this square with grid lines so that 16 or 24 smaller squares are marked off. Draw a similar grid on a piece of paper to record results.

Prepare a dish of crushed ice and a dish of very hot water. Put several nails with a sharp point into each dish. Blind-fold yourself or keep your eyes closed while your partner is experimenting on your hand.

Tweezers will be needed to pick a nail out of the hot water. Your partner will apply the point of a nail lightly in one of the squares of the grid. You will respond by describing the sensation as hot, cold, or just touch. The experimenter should select a hot or cold nail at random so that you cannot anticipate a sensation. Continue until all grid squares have been touched with both hot and cold nails. Examine the record of responses. What can you explain about the nerve ending in your palm? Try this experiment on a section of skin on your forearm, top of the foot, center of the back, etc. Which areas are most sensitive for hot, cold, or touch?

CHECKING THE TEMPERATURE RECEPTORS IN SKIN

Fill three dishes with water at different temperatures. In one put crushed ice until a thermometer reads 5°C or 40°F. In a second dish pour water that has been standing at room temperature, 25°C or 77°F. In the third dish pour water that has been heated to 45°C or 112°F.

Immerse your left hand in the cold water and your right hand in the hot water. Leave them there for a minute or two. What happens to your sensation of cold and heat? Which hand adjusts faster? Quickly put both hands in the dish at room temperature. What sensations do you feel now in each hand? The sensations of hot and cold are not exact. They depend upon how fast your skin loses or gains heat.

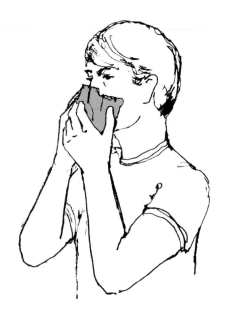

microscope and put a drop from the soapy jar on a slide you will notice the dirt clinging to the tiny droplets of oil. A clean skin is usually a healthy skin.

MAKING PRINTS OF YOUR FEET

Mix a teaspoon of baking soda with half a cup of water. Use cotton to wet the bottom of one foot completely with the solution. Stand carefully on the wet foot in the center of white paper. Hold the footprint six inches above a candle flame and warm the paper carefully.

If your arches are in good shape, the print will be narrow from the center back to the heel. A "flat foot" makes a print that is almost the same width from toes to heel.

Check out your shoe size. Draw around your shoe on a piece of paper. Put your weight on that bare foot and draw around it. Is there room for your foot in your shoe without squeezing it?

CLEANING YOUR SKIN

When the pores in your skin become filled with dirt and other foreign materials, pimples and blackheads will form. Take a closer look at your skin. Hold a magnifying lens in front of a mirror and look at your pores. These little openings lead to oil glands or sweat glands. Oil is necessary to keep the skin from drying out. Dirt sticks to it and needs to be washed away.

Fill two test tubes or small bottles one-quarter full of water. Pour in any kind of liquid cooking oil until the containers are half full. Into one tube add a little liquid soap. Shake both containers. What are the results? How does washing with soap get rid of the dirt? Repeat the above experiment, only this time add a small amount of soil to each. Shake each and observe again. If you have a

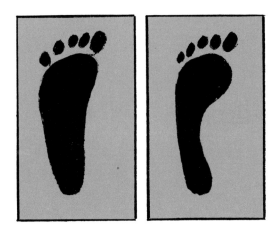

MAKING PRINTS
OF YOUR FINGERS

With the side of a pencil lead, make a heavy dark spot on a piece of paper. Rub your finger on this spot. Press your finger carefully onto the sticky side of a piece of cellophane tape. Fasten the tape to a piece of white paper so that the print shows clearly.

The inner layer of the skin or dermis has projections which fit into corresponding ridges in the outer layer of skin or epidermis. Sometimes these projections or knobs are arranged in rows, as on the tips of the fingers. This makes it possible to make a print of a finger. It is said that no two fingerprints are exactly alike, so fingerprints are helpful in identifying people.

USING URINALYSIS
TECHNIQUES

Purchase a roll of glucose test strips used by diabetics for the home testing of urine. You will also need a roll of pHydrion paper to check acidity.

Collect a small amount of urine in a disposable plastic cup. Dip the end of a two-inch strip of the test tape into the urine. Remove it and wait one minute. If the tape remains yellow there is no sugar in the urine. Most rolls include a color chart to indicate percent of concentration. Follow directions carefully before making a final comparison. Different products vary on the timing of a reading. The color changes from yellow to shades of green to almost black as the glucose concentration increases. A more accurate analysis for glucose can be done with clinitest tablets or Labstix reagent strips.

Usually urine is around pH 6, slightly acid. Dip a strip of pHydrion paper in urine and check the degree. The range on pH paper goes from 1 to 14; 7 is neutral, above 7 is alkaline, and below is acidic.

DEFINITIONS

acid — any of a group of chemical compounds that taste sour, turn blue litmus red, and can neutralize bases.

alkaline — containing a soluble salt or any base; will neutralize acids; alkaline chemicals turn red litmus blue.

glucose — a simple sugar found in honey and many fruits, only half as sweet as ordinary table sugar.

urinalysis — examining urine through a microscope or by doing chemical tests.

Appendix

Chapter 1

SEEING THE EFFECT OF YEAST ON DOUGH page 9

Yeast is a simple plant in the fungi group that lacks chlorophyll. Yeast cannot manufacture its own food. As these plants grow and reproduce they need sugar. In the bread dough without this compound the yeast cells did not have food and will not give off the carbon dioxide that causes dough to rise.

Chapter 2

COUNTING THE PROBABILITY OF INCOMPLETE DOMINANCE page 17

Chromosomes come in pairs. If we use C to represent color, than a kidney bean that is homozygous for red would be written CC. A white navy bean can be labeled as cc. When these two are crossed all the plants or offspring would get a C from the kidney bean parent and a c from the navy bean parent. Since neither one is dominant all offspring would have Cc and the color would be pink. You can prove this by having a bag of each type of bean. Pick one from each to illustrate an offspring. Every selection will end up with a pink combination, one white and one red.

When you mix all beans together you are using only the pink parents. As you randomly select two beans at a time you will end up with a ratio close to 50% pink, 25% red, and 25% white. This is what Mendel proposed over a century ago. He used red and white sweet peas. The above activity is a simulation of his. Red and white gumdrops or other objects can be used instead of the beans.

Chapter 3

PROVIDING RAW MATERIALS FOR PHOTOSYNTHESIS page 22

As baking soda dissolves in water carbon dioxide is given off. When soda is added to water an aquatic plant will photosynthesize at a faster rate. As a green plant manufactures sugar it releases oxygen. This gas is in the tiny bubbles given off from the cut end of the Elodea.

TESTING GASES PLANTS GIVE UP page 23

When you held the lighted match over the test tube that was in the light, the flame glowed brighter for oxygen is a by-product of photosynthesis. The gas escaping from the test tube in the dark will put out the flame. In the dark, plants give off carbon dioxide during the process of respiration.

Appendix

DETERMINING THE ROLE OF CHLOROPHYLL page 24

The green and maroon areas will turn bluish-black. The maroon color is a combination of green and pink pigments. They have chlorophyll which has made sugar. This compound is changed into starch. The pink and white regions lack chlorophyll and remain the brown tone of iodine.

DETERMINING HOW MUCH SOIL PLANTS USE page 25

The weight of the soil before and after a plant has grown in it will be close to the same figure. Plants use up only traces of minerals. Their extensive growth is made possible by making their own food from inorganic materials, water from the soil and carbon dioxide from the air.

GETTING RAW MATERIAL INTO A PLANT page 26

Green plants use water and carbon dioxide to make sugar. Water comes up through vessels and tracheids from the roots. The gas must get into the leaves through microscopic pores. Most land plants have the stoma or holes on the undersides of leaves. The two leaves which had their stoma on the underside clogged with vaseline will eventually die. The one with the coating on the upper side only will remain healthy.

OBSERVING TRANSPIRATION page 27

As water and minerals move from the soil into roots, up the stem, and out the petiole to the leaf, only part of this water is used to make food. The excess osmoses into the intercellular spaces around tiny pores or stoma, usually on the under surface of the leaf. High temperatures, low humidity, and wind currents increase the rate of transpiration. On a still, cool, cloudy humid day this process is slowed down.

EXPERIMENTING WITH CAPILLARITY AND WATER COHESION page 28

Water molecules adhere to the molecules of the material above it—the blotter, glass tube, sugar, lamp wick, and vessels in the xylem of the celery. This pull is greater than the cohesion or sticking together of one water molecule to the adjoining water molecule.

TESTING DIFFUSION page 29

Molecules of matter are always in motion. The molecules of one substance will move into another. When two compounds are confined in a glass, as in this experiment, the constant moving will eventually equalize into a uniform concentration. Diffusion occurs in all living cells of plants and animals.

OBSERVING OSMOSIS page 30

When two solutions are separated by a thin membrane, the more dilute solution will pass through it and move into the more concentrated solution if the membrane is permeable to it. If a membrane separates two different solutions of the same concentration, osmosis occurs in both directions if the molecules can go through the membrane. This process continues until equilibrium is reached and the solutions are identical.

DISCOVERING HOW PLANTS REACT page 32

Tropisms in plants are caused by auxins or growth hormones. They are produced in the tips of stems and roots. In sunlight auxin moves to the shady side of the stem, causing cell elongation and the stem leans toward the light (phototropism). Auxin in the root tip promotes a positive geotropic response.

Root tips will grow toward water but away from copper. When the tip is cut off the auxins are removed and the cut root grows right into the copper and dies.

DISCOVERING THE AREAS OF MITOSIS IN STEMS AND ROOTS page 35

The distance between the ink marks at the tip of the root and stem will get wider. Only the very tip of roots does the growing. It is covered by a cap of epidermal cells for protection as the root pushes through the soil. At the opposite end the terminal and lateral buds contain the meristematic tissue. These cells are dividing by mitosis. The ink marks at the top end of the seedling's stem will get farther apart while those near the root will remain the same.

TESTING THE EFFECT OF HEAT AND LIGHT ON GERMINATION page 36

The plants in the warm control dish should grow better than those in ice water. However, in the second test the plants in the dark may germinate faster. Light is not necessary for germination otherwise we wouldn't be able to plant seeds down in the dark soil.

Chapter 5

REGENERATING
ANIMALS page 50

A planarian cut into two or three pieces can regenerate itself. Each piece grows into a whole animal.

A planarian cut into five sections illustrates the anterior-posterior gradient. This means that the front end of the animal regenerates more rapidly and accurately. The first three pieces will grow into whole animals. The fourth section back grows a stump of a head and the tail piece has lost the ability to grow anything resembling the anterior end.

Humans can regenerate tissues such as the healing of wounds and the mending of bones. Only recently it was reported that a young girl in England did regenerate the tip of a finger that was cut off.

Chapter 7

EXPERIMENTING WITH
AN ENZYME page 59

Pepsin must be in a slightly acid medium to actively function as an enzyme to split up protein of egg white into polypeptides. Neither the enzyme nor acid alone can do the job. Extreme heat disrupts enzymatic action. In test tube #4 all the conditions were right for protein digestion. The size of the egg white should be much smaller than those in the other four test tubes.

DISCOVERING SOME
FUNCTIONS
OF THE SKIN page 61

It takes fat tissue longer to get cold than muscle tissue. Once the tissues reached the same temperature you probably found out that fat retains the cold longer than muscle.

The skin on plants and animals keeps them from dehydrating and prevents foreign materials from entering. The peeled fruits and vegetables will shrivel up and are attacked by fungi and bacteria.

TESTING FOR
VITAMIN C page 64

Vitamin C has a tendency to dissipate into the air. Juice from a freshly squeezed orange will be higher in Vitamin C than juice left in the refrigerator for several days. Boiling or the addition of bicarbonate of soda reduces the quantity of vitamin C in fruits. Consider all variables before drawing conclusions from your tests.

EMULSIFYING FATS   page 65

Except for a slight change of color nothing happens in test tube number one. In test tube number 2 it is apparent that oil and water do not mix. The oil floats on top of the water. The third test tube should demonstrate that bile emulsifies oil, breaking it up physically into tiny droplets which are suspended throughout the liquid. This increases the surface area of the oil to speed up the chemical action of enzymes that break down fat into fatty acids and glycerol. The gall bladder stores quantities of bile to be released into the small intestine when food is present. If it is removed the amount of bile secreted by the liver at any one time is very small. A person must limit the amount of greasy foods, fats, or oils consumed at one meal.

TESTING CHEMICALS
IN EXHALED AIR   page 66

The carbon dioxide in exhaled air chemically reacts with the blue solution (BTB) changing it first to green and then to yellow. An aquatic plant immersed in a solution of BTB and placed under a light will carry on photosynthesis. In this process carbon dioxide is necessary and will be removed from the solution. After a few hours the yellow liquid returns to its original blue color.

Clear limewater will turn milky when carbon dioxide is bubbled into it. It chemically reacts with the lime to form a precipitate, calcium carbonate.

DEMONSTRATING
ABSORPTION IN THE
SMALL INTESTINE   page 68

Pancreatic enzymes include lipase which breaks down fats, amylase which works on carbohydrates, and trypsin which reacts with proteins. Since the meal in the experiment contained all three basic foods your results should be positive for each test. Sugar, amino, acid and fatty acid will osmose through the tubing.

TESTING THE STRENGTH
OF CARDIAC MUSCLE   page 69

If your heart averaged 70 beats each minute and you lived for 75 years, the following figures are the totals for each time period:

4,200 per hour
100,000 per day
705,600 per week
2,822,400 per month
33,868,800 per year
2,540,160,000 in a lifetime

TESTING YOUR EARS page 71

When air waves are striking both eardrums or tympanic membranes one is able to pick up sounds more easily and to determine the direction of the sound. Since the molecules of matter are closer together in a solid than in a liquid or gas a sound is magnified.

FIGURING OUT THE JOB OF THE IRIS page 73

Covering the eyes causes the iris to relax and the pupils to become large. Bright light causes contraction and the openings are reduced. The ring of muscle fibers in each eye work independently of each other. The pupils of the eyes enlarge when one focuses on a distant object. The light reflected from close objects is usually more intense and the iris contracts more.

STIMULATING YOUR REFLEXES page 76

When the tendon just below he kneecap is tapped the lower leg will swing upward. Even when one concentrates on preventing this reflex it is difficult to stop the action.

Acid foods stimulate digestive glands to release their juices and enzymes. Tart appetizers improve digestion. The hunger center in the brain is inhibited as the level of sugar in the blood rises.

The kinesthetic or muscle sense is not as accurate on fine movements without the assistance of vision.

The semicircular canals in the inner ear assist you in maintaining your balance. Seeing objects in relation to yourself is necessary for good posture. When the eyes are closed one tends to lean or sway.

Most people cannot stop themselves from getting "goose pimples," blushing, or sneezing, for these actions are not under the control of the central or somatic nervous system.

LOCATING YOUR BLIND SPOT page 77

The optic nerve enters the back of the eyeball and spreads out to form the inside coat called the retina. This layer is composed of nervous tissues called rods which pick up black and white and cones which pick up color. The point at which the nerve enters the eye is the blind spot. When an image crosses this juncture nothing is visible.

Index

Index

Index

Helen J. Challand earned her M.A. and Ph.D. from Northwestern University. She currently is Chair of the Science Department at National College of Education and Coordinator of Undergraduate Studies for the college's West Suburban Campus.

An experienced classroom teacher and science consultant, Dr. Challand has worked on science projects for Scott Foresman and Company, Rand McNally Publishers, Harper-Row Publishers, Encyclopedia Britannica Films, Coronet Films, and Journal Films. She is associate editor for the *Young People's Science Encyclopedia* published by Childrens Press.